GROUNDING CO

by Stephanie Siege

CW01499381

What does it do?

Grounding yourself can help bring you into the here and now. It can make you feel stronger and more stable.

Who is it useful for?

Absolutely anyone can benefit from grounding.

Introduction

I was a scatterbrain and a space cadet whenever anything triggered my traumas. I found that almost every interaction with people did just that. This grounding technique was one of the very first skills I learned in clairvoyance classes, back in 1997.

After my first weekend intensive, as I got into my car to leave, I slammed my car door shut, and the handle literally came off in my hand! It had been jiggly but had shown no sign of breaking beforehand. I immediately recognized the power I had in my body, as a result of that class.

Of course, I did not stay grounded all the time, for being ungrounded was my habit of 30-odd years. Changing a habitual behavior that happens every single second requires patience, amusement, and self-compassion. So by 2023, am I grounded every single second? No. But I am grounded a lot more often than I was before.

Defining Grounding

To ground, I don't have to stand barefoot on soil, (although it is nice, especially on a warm beach). I can sit in my house and still connect to the earth. How is that possible? The connection is not physical, it is energetic. This kind of energy passes through floors, walls, and everything. You can even ground from the 50th floor or from an airplane.

How grounding works:

In most houses today, each electrical outlet on the wall has three wires behind it. One wire carries a current of electricity from your electrical panel (sometimes called a breaker box) to the outlet. The second wire carries electricity back to the electrical panel. The third wire carries excess electricity to the ground for safety. Earth can absorb extra energy without being harmed, but your appliances cannot.

Now wouldn't it be great for your body-mind-spirit to have a grounding wire—a mechanism to remove excess energy so that you don't get frazzled, fried, or burned out like the smoking black shell of a charred hair dryer? Here it is!

Technique:

1. Sit up in a chair with your feet flat on the floor (not crossed).

2. Visualize something long and vertical, like an electrical wire, a plumbing pipe, a water slide, a tree trunk, an alabaster column, a tail, or whatever you'd like.

3. Imagine it standing in front of you, as a tree trunk would.

4. Now, lengthen it. Make it long enough to reach down all the way to the center of the earth. Don't look up the number of miles. Don't huff and puff as if you might get

it wrong. It's easy peasy.

5. Now imagine that your item—I'm going to call it a grounding cord—is just beneath where you sit. While your physical body sits on a chair, your energy body sits on your grounding cord. Of course, you can make it comfortable and cushy. Definitely make it more than wide enough to accommodate your physical body.

6. It must seem sturdy to you. Being packed into 3,958.8 miles of earth seems sturdy to me.

7. When you're connected to this sturdy, grounding item, you are sturdy too. Your body actually has energy centers along the spine. The lowest of those is almost at the bottom tip of the spine or tailbone. The energy center is disk-shaped like a coin, about the size of a U.S. quarter or half-dollar coin. It faces forward. Your grounding cord can come all the way up to that disk. The cord connects to the disk like a powerful electromagnet, or whatever you see as a secure connection. When you sit down to ground yourself, you may find that your energy field contains, say, snarky energy from some old primary school playmate. You can command that energy to enter that tailbone energy center and proceed downward, as if by gravity, all the way down to the center of the Earth. You see, with this marvelous meditation, you can practice letting go of what is not serving you.

8. Give the "release" command and watch what happens. You might see in your mind's eye some faces, places, or incidents floating by, on their way out. You might feel an emotion-stirring or not. The process works even when you don't feel or see anything.

9. After releasing energy, decide that clean, pure, life energy is now filling up all empty spaces in your energy body.

10. If you remember, you can put on a grounding cord whenever you sit down. When you stand up and walk around, it can go with you. Your grounding cord can also accompany you to bed and to sleep.

11. If you forget about your grounding cord and don't see it anymore, you can make a new one. Just remember to clean up after yourself. Here's how: decide that the old one, wherever it may be, drops into Mother Earth's Recycling Center at the center of the Earth.

12. Try this out a few times this week. Notice whether anything changes in your perceptions, feelings, and interactions.

Feel free to let me know at: https://www.facebook.com/stephanie.siegel.14/ or https://www.Facebook.com/PayAttentionforFallPrevention

Tips for using this technique with a client

If you, as a coach, practice this grounding exercise every day, you will in turn be in alignment (walking your talk), if you decide to teach a client about grounding. They will learn hundreds of times more from your example than from your words. I recommend you do this grounding exercise and be sure you are staying grounded for at least 10 minutes before you meet with the client. Heck, why not before every client? You don't have to teach about grounding to model it.

Also, you'll probably think faster and communicate more clearly when grounded. If you usually think fast and clearly, you probably are grounded most of the time already. Trees don't need a grounding cord technique; they are naturally grounded. If you're like that, you might need a technique only when a surprise attack or disappointment *"knocks you off your feet,"* or *"pulls the rug out from under you,"* as the sayings go. If you practice it for a few minutes every day, you'll have it when you need it.

Great for:
Regaining composure after something bamboozles you. Practicing it regularly might even prevent some bamboozlement!

If you'd like to listen to this exercise, check out my 5-minute video at https://www.facebook.com/100002197638543/videos/280443264872714

Stephanie Siegel

Qualifications/ Services Offered: Clairvoyant coach, reader, healer, teacher, speaker, author

Facebook: https://www.facebook.com/stephanie.siegel.14/

LinkedIn: https://www.LinkedIn.com/in/eagleeyesiegel

Location: online, and from Atlanta, Georgia, USA

Stephanie Siegel is a clairvoyant, spiritual healer, teacher and author. She teaches psychics and sensitives how to manage their clairaudience, telepathy, clairsentience (empathy), and mediumship abilities to have a calmer life. For senior citizens, she teaches the use of everyday mindfulness in Pay Attention for Fall Prevention℠ classes. Stephanie's intuitive readings shine a light on the next step of a person's spiritual journey and sometimes lead to amazing healing.

Her psychic studies in this lifetime began in 1997 in the clairvoyant methods taught at the Berkeley Psychic Institute. Stephanie is ordained and certified to teach in this nondenominational mystical tradition.

Stephanie has a master's degree in journalism from the University of Missouri and had a full-time writing and editing career at CNN.com, WebMD, the US Centers for Disease Control and Prevention (CDC), The Atlanta Journal-Constitution, and other newspapers and websites. She also has served five fussy felines in succession.

Now she writes articles and stories for adults and children about confidence, intuition, and other spiritual abilities. Her book projects include historical fiction about a soul's series of incarnations, and a fun nonfiction book about how cats will out-intuit you, paws down.

YOU ARE WHAT YOU EAT

by Cornelia Kawann

What does it do?

It empowers moms, entrepreneurs, and biohackers who do not want to follow nutrition trends and fancy diets, to use a powerful tool to communicate with their bodies. This empowers them to eat in harmony with their bodies and experience how it will truly benefit their health and well-being.

Who's it useful for?

- People who are mindful about their nutrition.
- Busy entrepreneurs, who despite their packed schedules, would like to treat their bodies with healthy food.
- Moms who want to nurture their families with healthy food.
- Biohackers who want to check out a new powerful tool that literally changes their lives and health.

DO YOU KNOW WHAT IS GOOD FOR YOUR BODY?

Hardly anything is talked and written about as much as nutrition, dieting, and weight loss. There are so many recommendations that it is difficult to keep track, particularly because recommendations are continually in flux. Do you feel the same way? What is food for you?

Food can fulfil a variety of roles and needs, such as:

- Repletion and overcoming the feeling of being hungry
- Problem solver
- Distraction
- Pleasure
- Source of energy

When you eat natural, whole foods, and drink lots of clean, fresh water, you enhance your personal life energy. For me, food is concentrated, intelligent energy that nourishes my body, mind and spirit. From an energetic perspective, a balanced diet does not evolve around fat, carbohydrates, proteins, calories and vitamins. The goal is not to follow nutrition trends and fancy diets but to support your body to get the nutrition it truly needs. But do you actually KNOW what your body needs? Or do you THINK you know what it needs?

This is actually THE most important aspect of nutrition that is scarcely spoken of. The critical information lies in knowing whether what you are eating or drinking is good for YOUR body. We are all unique and so are our bodies. Hence, even if science is telling you that this is healthy for you, you don't really know if this is true for your unique body. The only expert who knows what is good for your body is your body itself and only your body. Your body knows exactly what it NEEDS right now and what is good for it. This raises the next question: How do YOU know what is good for your body?

This chapter revolves around how to find out which nutrition is the best for YOU, and specifically nutrition in the energetic sense. Hence, you will learn how you can communicate with your body to find out what nutrition it needs, and when. Through this process, you will learn to eat in harmony with your body and experience how it will truly benefit you.

Are you ready to start communicating with your body? Ok, let's get started.

HAVE YOU EVER HEARD OF BOVIS?

When I started working with my personal energy, there was one thing that puzzled me as an electrical engineer: why was there no unit to measure personal energy? We cannot see and hear electrical energy but we can measure it in kWh. Hence, I was convinced, if it is possible to measure electrical energy, then it must also be possible to measure personal energy.

After much research, I finally uncovered a way to measure personal energy and that there is actually a unit with which, you can measure life energy. This unit is called Bovis and owes its name to the French radiesthesist, Andre Bovis (1871-1947). In the 1930s, his goal was to develop a simple quality control for food. With this method, he wanted to quickly and easily measure the freshness and vitality of food and to have an indicator of the beneficial value of that food for the human body.

Based on his observations and experiments, Andre Bovis developed a scale with values between 1 and 10'000 Bovis. He found that a value of 7'000 Bovis should be the minimum for health and food. The main points of the Bovis scale are as follows:

01 The lower the value of an object on the Bovis scale, the worse it is for your body.

02 Everything that has more than 7'000 Bovis can have a supportive effect on your organism.

03 Everything below 7'000 Bovis takes energy away from your body.

04 Food and substances below 3'000 Bovis are even extremely detrimental.

These are the values of the original Bovis scale, but now the scale is set to open upwards. Andre Bovis used a pendulum to assess the Bovis scale. Here, I am going to show you how you can use your body as a pendulum. This knowledge has served as a powerful tool that literally changed my life.

GET TO KNOW THE STANDING METHOD

The easiest way to measure your life energy is with the kinesiological muscle test. This method originates with its founder, Dr. George Goodheart. He was an American chiropractor who, in the course of his work, discovered the connection between muscle tension and our thoughts, feelings and beliefs. The body reacts to positive impulses with muscle strength, and to negative impulses with muscle weakness. This method works because our body cannot lie.

There are different ways you can use the kinesiological muscle test, however, the easiest way is with the Standing Method. As a wonderful self-help tool, this method is unique in that it is simple to use and that you can do it all by yourself. In this Chapter, I am going to show you how to use the Standing Method to measure your energy.

In order to use the kinesiological muscle test and to communicate with your body, you need to calibrate your body first. You can do this with the following Energy Tool #1.

Energy Tool #1

CALIBRATING THE STANDING METHOD

01 Stand up. Place your feet hip-width apart.

02 Place your left hand on your belly button and your right hand over it.

03 Now close your eyes and concentrate on your inner center.

04 Now ask the following question (loud): "Body please show me a clear YES". Pay attention to how your body reacts to this question and notice what you have perceived.

05 Now ask the following question (loud): "Body please show me a clear NO". Again. pay attention to how your body reacts to this question and notice what you have perceived.

According to the movements of your body, you now know your "YES" and your "NO".

With 90% of all people your body tilts:

a little bit forward for a "YES"

a little bit backwards for a "NO"

However, your body's answers can also be the opposite, or cover an array of alternate possibilities. For example, your body might not move at all as an answer, or perhaps it moves to the side. To discover your body's response, stay centered and calm, while concentrating on the movements of your body.

After you know what your "YES" and "NO" look like, write them down, as this is essential to know for any further communication.

HOW TO MEASURE YOUR LIFE ENERGY

Before you can find out which foods are actually good for you, you must know how to measure your own Bovis value. Now that you know how to use the Standing Method, let's measure how much personal energy you have in Bovis. The goal in knowing your Bovis value is not that you have the exact number of your own energy, but rather to know what kind of food and environment is good for you. By measuring the Bovis values of the food you are eating and comparing it to your own Bovis value, you learn if it is giving you energy or taking energy from you, with the help of Energy Tool #2.

Energy Tool #2

MEASURE YOUR BOVIS VALUES

01 Stand up. Place your feet hip-width apart.

02 Close your eyes.

03 Ask (loud): "How many Bovis do I have?"

04 Ask (loud): "Is the value above 5'000?" YES?

05 Ask (loud): "Is the value above 6'000?" YES?

06 Continue to ask this question until you get a NO.

07 The number before you get a NO is your personal Bovis value.

When you are testing your Bovis value for the first time, you can fine-tune it by reducing the steps. Let's say you get a NO at 9'000 Bovis. Then you can continue to ask: Is the value above 8'500 Bovis? If you get a "YES" you can continue from there until you get your next "NO". Let's say you get it at 8'700. Then you can continue to ask: Is the value above 8'650? If you get a "YES" then you can narrow it down from there.

The first time you do this, it might take a bit longer to determine your Bovis value. However, as you familiarize yourself with the process, it will become increasingly quick and easy. The personal energy of a healthy person is, on average, around 7 '500 Bovis. What is your Bovis value right now?

MEASURE IF FOOD IS SUITABLE FOR YOU

The next step is to find out which foods are good for your body. If you nurture your body with food that has more Bovis than your body (e.g., more than 7'000 Bovis), then you are supplying your body with energy and foods that empower you. Therefore, it is important to be able to determine for yourself, which foods supply your body with vital energy and which do not. You can determine it easily with Energy Tool #3, a fun and engaging process that can bring much insight into your life!

01 Stand up. Place your feet hip-width apart.

02 Close your eyes. Think of the food you are holding in your hand or standing in front of you.

03 Ask (loud): "Does this food have more Bovis values than me? Does it give me energy?"

04 If you get a YES - go ahead and enjoy our food.

05 If you get a NO - you can change its energy by saying: "I bless this food with divine energy!"

06 Check again by asking (loud): "Does this food have more Bovis values than me? Does it give me energy?"

07 If you get a YES now - enjoy your food!
If you still get a NO - I wouldn't eat it.

The ability to test whether or not something is good for you can massively simplify your life. A couple of years ago, I listened to an interview with Anthony Williams. He maintains that one of the healthiest foods on Earth is freshly squeezed celery juice. Perhaps you have heard of it too? Since I like to integrate new biohacks into my life, I immediately bought a juicer. From then on, every morning I made fresh celery juice and drank it. However, I eventually noticed that after drinking celery juice, I consistently ended up with a stomach ache.

Despite being a bit late, I tested whether the celery juice was good for me and my body. The answer was clear: NO, it was not good for my body at that time (if only I had done this before I bought a juicer! 😊).

Cornelia's Tip:

ONLY EAT FOOD THAT DOES YOU GOOD

Now that I know how to fuel my body only with what serves me, I am much more mindful of what I eat, where food comes from, and if it gives my body energy. Most of the time we are well aware of what we should eat and what we shouldn't. Often, we give in to temptation and eat it anyway because it looks so tasty. Now that you know how to check in with your body, eating becomes a more conscious decision. Sometimes you may eat against your body's wisdom, this is ok, but remember that you always have a choice. You can reframe the question as follows: do I love my body enough to NOT eat this doughnut, for example? Try it out! The results are very powerful.

Cornelia Kawann

Electrical Engineer – Personal Energy Strategist

Cornelia Kawann is an executive in the Swiss electricity regulator and the founder of *energy-on!*

During her corporate career, she has held various management positions in several energy companies in Europe, all the while founding two start-ups.

As a Personal Energy Strategist under the brand *energy-on!,* Cornelia empowers busy female exec-preneurs to use their full energy and thrive in their career and business.

As an electrical engineer, working with energy and frequencies in all its forms comes naturally to her. She explains to her clients the world of quantum physics and shows them how to understand, measure, increase and shift their energy. Managing their own energy is the shortcut to reaching their goals.

When not working in the energy industry or with private clients, Cornelia can be found sharing her hacks in her *energy-on!* show, or interviewing inspiring energy workers and scientists. She also often appears on podcasts as a guest and at international conferences as a speaker.

During her studies, she won scholarships at two American Universities and later worked at the Lawrence Berkeley Laboratory, and in several energy companies in Europe. All these different touch points resulted in a vast global network.

Cornelia's mission is to make energy work popular. Her passions include painting, swimming long distances, and visiting places with high energy. She stems from an Austrian family of entrepreneurs, which is why building companies and problem-solving is in her DNA.

Within 3 months she had written an outstanding book about Personal Energy Management with which she shares all her wisdom, empowering other women to do the same and to have all the energy to make their dreams come true.

HOW TO HONOR AND CONNECT WITH EMOTIONS: A GUIDE TO REGULATING THE NERVOUS SYSTEM

by Lauren Vaknine

This exercise :

I was diagnosed with Juvenile Rheumatoid Arthritis before my second birthday. I was wheelchair-bound with no use of any joint in my body by the age of 18, at which point, I made a choice that disability wouldn't be my story; wellness would.

At 29, I went into remission.

This was not a linear journey. Once I decided that I was going to heal, I inevitably began with the physical modalities. They were great and they were needed. Our bodies, after all, are the convergence place between the 3D reality we see, and the quantum realities we cannot perceive with our human minds. Our bodies are the vessels through which we carry out our work as cosmic beings. However, I was mistaken to think that my healing required a solely somatic approach. Once the physical healing only got me so far in my quest for remission, I realized I also needed to address the mental, emotional and spiritual.

What I have noticed in the years since my remission, through myself and hundreds of clients, is that we either ignore our emotions in order to distract ourselves from the challenging feelings they bring up, or we let them define and control us.

As a result, I created a process I call "Honoring & Processing

Emotions", as a way to fully feel and honor any emotion that surfaces, while allowing ourselves the opportunity to process the emotion through and out of the body. We maintain our personal power by fully processing our emotions. Unprocessed emotions get stuck both physically and spiritually, which causes us to vibrate at a lower energetic frequency, which in turn, is counterproductive to healing, manifestation, and our spiritual evolution.

Everything in the Universe holds an energetic frequency. Our thoughts and emotions are not exempt. The Hawkins Scale of Consciousness shows us that emotions such as shame, fear, guilt and grief vibrate at very low frequencies, of between 20 to 100. On this level, we are operating solely within the third dimension and from the lower ego self, which is a place of victim consciousness, where no healing or elevation is possible. Love, on the other hand, vibrates at a frequency of 500. But acceptance comes in at 350, which shows us that even by moving ourselves out of grief and shame and into acceptance, we raise our energetic vibration to something more resonant with wellness. This is why processing our emotions is potentially more powerful than measures we take to aid the *physical* body back to health.

We cannot discount the importance of **unearthing** and **releasing** repressed emotions as a way of preventing illness, healing trauma, moving into a state of positive mental health, and deepening our spiritual connection.

If you ignore your pain, hide it, suppress it, or avoid it, you only increase it. To be able to *heal*, you have to first *feel*.

Emotional Intelligence expert Sean Grover calls this "passing through the doorway of grief". We have to give ourselves permission to grieve and express our feelings, without judging ourselves for them. Then we need to find a way to let them pass through and out of the body, in order that they no longer hold us back physically, *and* energetically.

Below is my 6-step process for honoring and processing emotions. You can use this process as a tool to manage a challenging situation, experience or trauma. If you are a practitioner, this is one of the most potent ways to empower your client/patients to effectively manage their emotions. Among the many tools and exercises available to my clients within my Recondition Your Life Academy course, this is by far the most used, and favorite.

1. Acknowledge

The first part of the process of honoring our emotions is to acknowledge the emotion fully. When we feel a heightened emotion, we often try to escape it. Even if we cry and thereby assume we've "got it all out", we generally forget to actually process the emotion. We assume that the act of crying is a sufficient way to process. Or perhaps we cry, and then distract ourselves with work and say something like, "I gave myself some time to cry, and now I'm going to crack on". Instead, rather than distracting ourselves from the emotion, we must feel the emotion *fully*. We must allow the emotion to communicate the reason for its existence. For part 1, start by simply sitting with the emotion and allowing it to do what it needs to do. Ask the emotion why it is present and what it is here to tell you. Ask the emotion what it wants you to feel, and why. Let the emotion speak to you.

2. Locate & Express

Notice where in your body the emotion is located. Is it in your chest, your stomach, your throat, or your neck? Once you have located it, put your hand there and then give the emotion a name/word (for example, are you feeling unappreciated, insulted, hurt, not understood, angry, or let down?). Allow yourself to name the emotion in its location. Each time you do this exercise, notice whether different emotions are located in different places in the body. For example, work-related stress might be localized to the throat, romantic challenges in the stomach, and challenges with family in the heart. This is simply an example, it will be different for everyone.

3. Immerse

Now it's time to give yourself **permission** to feel this emotion fully. Feel *all of it;* allow it to wash over you totally. This isn't wallowing. We're giving ourselves full permission without judgment to feel the emotion, for the very reason that once we've fully acknowledged and honored the emotion, it will be easier to move it out of the body. The alternative is that it remains stagnant in our energy system, which is what happens when we don't fully honor it. This often results in physical illness and a heightened sense of anxiety and mental distress.

4. "It Hurts Here"

Now, with your hand still on the place where you have located the emotion, and with eyes closed, begin to say out loud "It hurts here, it hurts here". Say the phrase over and over until you feel you've given yourself enough time to honor how deeply it hurts. If you're aware of more than one location for the pain, move your hand from place to place. At every location, pause for a moment and express what you're feeling. When you experience physical discomfort, it means that something is unbalanced in your experience — physically, mentally, or spiritually. Your body knows it — every cell in your body knows it. Your body may well be processing a trauma before you've consciously accepted or acknowledged this trauma. Befriend these sensations and their wisdom, because the pain is actually leading you to wholeness.

5. Move the Emotion Through Your Body

Now, imagine that mass of emotion condensed into a little marble in the very place where you located it, and visualize yourself moving that marble through your body, until it comes out the bottom of your foot. It may take some force to move it through, it might not be a quick process, but allow your mind to do this in just the way it needs to. You can visualize kicking it into space and seeing it evaporating in space once it's out, if this helps you to energetically remove it from actuality.

6. Release the Emotion

Place your attention on the part of your body where you're holding the pain, and with every exhalation of your breath, have an intention of releasing that tension. For the next 30 seconds, just feel the painful sensation leaving your body with every breath. Some people find that making an audible tone that resonates in that part of your body where the pain is localized, helps to loosen and lift the contraction away. Animals physically shake themselves off after experiencing stress (like the threat of a predator). We are animals. This is the time to move. Put on some high-vibration music (ecstatic dance playlists are great), and move your body with absolutely no inhibitions to release this emotion from you fully. You may try deep breathing at the same time, using essential oils, and taking a long warm bath afterwards, as water energetically symbolizes new beginnings.

These 2 elements – an idea in the mind and a physical sensation in the body – are what an emotion really is – E Motion; Energy in Motion – and they can't be separated. This is why we call it a FEELING because we FEEL emotions in our body.

Other ways to process:

Cry into your Journal

This might sound bizarre, but it's a process that really works and is another way of allowing yourself to be immersed in the emotion. When you find yourself dealing with something that is really difficult, and you have all that pent-up emotion inside of you, take yourself somewhere you won't be disturbed, and journal – WHILE YOU CRY. Allow the tears to fall on the page. If you journal when the emotion is at its most heightened, you'll be very much led intuitively as you write, which will lead to a lot of clarity.

Take Responsibility

Be aware that any painful feelings you experience are *your* feelings. These feelings are happening inside your body now as you remember the pain, even though nothing is actually taking place in the material world. You are only remembering what happened, yet your body is reacting with muscle contractions, hormonal secretions, and other responses within you. Even when the painful incident was occurring in the material world, the effect was entirely within you. You have a choice in how you interpret and respond to emotional turbulence. Recognizing this is taking responsibility for your feelings.

This doesn't mean you feel guilty. Instead, it means you recognize your ability to respond to painful situations in new and creative ways. By taking responsibility for and honoring your feelings, you can also gain the power to make the pain melt away. You take back your personal power. You're no longer blaming anyone else for having caused the pain, so you no longer have to depend on anyone else to make it go away. Hold that understanding in your consciousness for the next few moments.

Celebrate the Process

Now you can celebrate the painful experience that has taken place. It is presented physically in you to awaken you to what needs to be released, and honoring it will move you to a higher level of consciousness. What was previously a disconnected, destructive, and disabled part of your psyche (in an attempt by your reptilian brain to "protect you"), is now integrated and contributing its power toward your greater spiritual goal. Instead of responding to the situation with a pain reflex and perpetuating the problem, you have turned it into an opportunity for spiritual transformation. That is something to celebrate!

Treat yourself by doing something that lights you up, or even buying yourself something that will make you happy.

Use these exercises whenever you feel upset, to free yourself from emotional turbulence and the underlying pain of any situation.

Lauren Vaknine

You can find Lauren on Instagram @laurenvaknine, on her podcast *Reconditioned with Lauren Vaknine*, and you can access all her offerings on her website www.laurenvaknine.co.uk

Email: lauren@laurenvaknine.co.uk

Tel: +44 (0) 7515 799 769

PA: clare@laurenvaknine.co.uk

Lauren Vaknine is a leading master holistic health and life coach, wellness educator, health writer, TED-X speaker and host of the popular *Reconditioned* Podcast. As a leading voice in wellness in the UK, Lauren uses the experience and knowledge she gained during her 3-decade journey from severe disability to complete wellness, to help women heal and transform their lives. She does this by using a range of holistic healing arts in a unique, whole-person approach that combines health optimisation, emotional alchemy, mental healing & spiritual development. This approach enables Lauren to take people from a life of struggle and mediocrity, to complete life optimisation. Aside from her extensive first-hand experience of healing, Lauren is also trained in NLP, CBT, EFT, nutrition, life coaching and Divine Feminine healing. Lauren believes that it makes no difference which aspect of your life you're hoping to uplevel, it all requires the same, whole-person approach.

"Wellness is not merely the absence of illness; it is the state of complete physical, mental, emotional & spiritual wellbeing."

- Lauren Vaknine

UNDERSTANDING OUR NIGHTMARES AND DISCOVERING THEIR HIDDEN GIFTS

by Andrea Morrison

1. What It Does

Connecting with our dreams can help us understand our subconscious minds on a deeper level, resulting in more peace and clarity in our waking lives. Nightmares are commonly viewed solely as scary dreams, but they often have the most potent messages of all. By understanding the messages from our nightmares, we can overcome mental blocks, trauma, anxiety, and unresolved issues. The subconscious barriers that hold us back are usually elusive, making our nightmares invaluable tools for unearthing these obstacles, and propelling us toward personal growth and transformation.

2. Great For People Who Are:

- Grappling with challenges, the underlying causes of which may not yet be apparent
- Experiencing recurring nightmares
- Suffering from insomnia or restless nights
- Wanting to uncover subconscious blocks to feel happier in their waking life
- Struggling from unresolved trauma
- Interested in lucid dreaming
- Seeking deeper self-awareness

3. Introduction: The Gift of Nightmares

Nightmare (n) - a frightening or unpleasant dream.

Nightmares, often seen as terrifying experiences through the shadowy landscapes of our subconscious, have long eluded true understanding. While they are typically associated with fear, discomfort, and darkness, there is actually a profound and often overlooked dimension to nightmares. Nightmares, when understood, can be the key to unlocking your subconscious mind.

Throughout my life, nightmares have played dual roles as both tormentors and invaluable teachers. Like many, I used to dread falling asleep and experiencing another nightmare, as well as the residual fear upon waking. However, after connecting with my dreams and learning how to interpret them, I've come to appreciate the hidden gifts that nightmares bring. Now, I navigate their dark characters and environment with curiosity rather than fear.

The misinterpretation of nightmares stems from the tendency to analyze them through the framework of our waking lives. These dreams are often dismissed as incoherent and frightening narratives, spun by our minds during sleep. In truth, they are invitations to explore our inner worlds, confront buried fears, and heal past wounds.

In Tibetan Dream Yoga, nightmares are considered messages that persist because we are "bad listeners." Each dream is believed to hold a lesson, and if we do not grasp its message, the dream intensifies in an effort to ensure remembrance. Nightmares, therefore, are the easiest to recall, as they beg for our understanding.

When we experience a nightmare, an ideal response is one of acceptance and embrace. This is the polar opposite of our usual reaction to nightmares that has generally persisted across our entire lives. In a complete paradigm shift, I encourage you to "hug the monster." The 'monster' represents any dark or scary dream symbol within your nightmare, *which is simply asking to be understood.*

As an example of how a nightmare can actually be healing, I will share a recent dream interpretation session. My client had a horrid and recurrent nightmare that has haunted her for years. In the nightmare, a boy she knew from summer camp long ago, was wearing a mask, holding a gun, and was targeting her family.

Through our interpretation, my client unveiled the symbolism hidden within the dream. She was raised in the quintessential nuclear family that adhered to societal norms. My client's true self, by contrast, is one of nonconformity, and one which she felt forced to conceal throughout her childhood. Together, we deduced that the boy wearing a mask symbolized my client hiding her true self. His act of shooting her family symbolized her readiness to shed her facade, and finally embrace her authentic, eccentric self.

While this may be an extremely intense way for her subconscious mind to convey this message, the fact that it was so scary, made it both memorable and easier to interpret. My client finally overcame this nightmare, embraced the boy (the monster), and is now applying this lesson to her family of husband and daughter. This insight into her subconscious and the healing that ensued has propelled her to encourage her daughter to always stay true to herself, regardless of societal norms or expectations. In this way, we can see how acknowledging and interpreting our dreams can lead to profound healing, even across generations.

In most instances, the most terrifying elements within our nightmares are simply parts of ourselves that have been neglected or misunderstood. They yearn for acknowledgement and understanding. By facing these inner "monsters" and offering them the attention and acceptance they crave, we unlock the ability to learn and heal.

4. Steps to Interpret and Connect with Nightmares

1. **Capture your nightmares:** The practice of remembering your dreams is key. Begin by keeping a dream journal. Record your dreams as soon as you wake up, noting every detail, emotion, and vivid image. This step is crucial in deciphering the recurring symbols and themes within your nightmares.

2. **Decode symbols:** Periodically, do an audit of your dream journal and dissect the symbolism within your nightmares. Identify recurring motifs, characters, or scenarios within the context of your life. These are not random, but rather, symbolic representations of your inner struggles and unmet needs.

3. **Connect with 'The Monster':** Enter a meditative state and revisit the nightmare in your mind. (If your nightmare is particularly potent or triggering, it's best to do this in the presence of a trusted and supportive companion.) Once you are mentally in your nightmare again, engage with the symbols and emotions you identified. Have a conversation with the monster and ask it questions, such as, "What do you need? Why are you here? What part of me is needing attention? What message do you have for me?" Listen carefully for answers

from your subconscious.

4. **Visualize the fear getting smaller:** Imagine anything that elicited fear in your nightmare, as a big ball in your mind. Slowly, make this ball smaller and smaller, to the point that it shrinks to the size of a pea. Now look at the small ball in your hand. Recognize that you have power over it, and that the fear no longer has control over you.

5. **Bring it to the light:** Now that you have interpreted your nightmare, it's time to integrate this newfound knowledge into your waking life. Ask yourself how these insights can inform your daily decisions, relationships, or actions. Use your responses as a compass for personal growth and transformation.

5. Tips for Coaches to Use with Clients

Here are some tips to assist clients in using nightmares as tools for self-discovery:

- **Create a safe space:** Ensure your clients feel safe and supported when sharing their nightmares. Establishing trust is crucial in this process. When clients share their dreams, they are sharing a deep part of their subconscious mind, which is a vulnerable process and may reveal more than they even realize.

- **Encourage journaling:** Suggest that clients keep a dream/nightmare journal. Regular recording of dreams can help identify patterns and recurring symbols.

- **Symbolic exploration:** Assist clients in interpreting the symbolism within their nightmares. Help them see the connections between dream symbols and their waking lives. Encourage them to trust their intuition rather than turning to a dream dictionary. Every person has a unique 'language' that they can learn to understand.

- **Message from 'the Monster':** If they are open to it, have your client role-play as the monster. Once both of you get into a meditative state, guide your client to take on the role of the 'monster,' and then have a conversation with them. Ask them questions and see what intuitively comes to the surface.

- **Integration techniques:** Guide clients in integrating their nightmare's insights into their daily lives. Encourage them to make conscious choices based on the wisdom gained from their dreams.

- **Life is a dream:** Tibetan dream yogis do not believe in a separation between our dreams and our waking lives - they believe that life *is* a dream. Adopting this perspective may allow your clients to decode the symbolism and meaning in everyday experiences more readily. Every person and interaction can be seen as a reflection of the subconscious mind, providing valuable insights for personal growth.

Nightmares are not to be feared but embraced. They are powerful tools for self-discovery, offering us a unique glimpse into the deepest parts of our subconscious minds. By following these steps and offering support, coaches can help clients unlock the transformative potential that lies within the darkness of their dreams.

Andrea Morrison

Dream + Life Coach & Business Alchemist
Host of Dream Life Connection Podcast

Website: dreamlifeconnection.com
Instagram: @dreamlifeconnection
Location: PNW/Global

Andrea is a professional dream interpreter, life coach, digital nomad, and podcaster. She guides people to connect with their dream lives: interpreting their night dreams and manifesting their daydreams. In addition to her expertise in dreamwork, Andrea specializes in mindset coaching, which she calls the "magic mindset." Through this transformative practice, she assists her clients in finding more joy and magic, as well as gaining the clarity and hope they need to create their dream lives easily.

Her podcast, *Dream Life Connection*, dives into personal development topics like dreamwork, modern magic, and mindset shifts. Similarly, her weekly newsletter, *Magic Monday*, shares modern magic tricks that bring inspiration and alignment into your life.

Beyond her work in personal development, Andrea doubles as a virtual business 'alchemist,' helping spiritual entrepreneurs grow their small businesses. She has a unique background of 8+ years in Creative Services at a major TV station; as a business consultant, she is able to blend her expertise in marketing with her passion for small businesses by mentoring and assisting her clients.

SOUL + SCIENCE = HEALING SYSTEM

by Sinead O'Hare

Trauma, the Brain, the Nervous System, and Healing

Unlock the power within you to heal from trauma and reclaim your life. Combining psychological science with spiritual principles, this chapter will guide you through actionable insights and proven methods to supercharge your healing journey.

Great for people who:

- Wish to understand the complex relationship between trauma, the brain, and the nervous system
- Aim to gain control over their lives by implementing practical psychological and spiritual healing techniques
- Are open to a holistic approach that blends science and spirituality
- Seek to become empowered through knowledge and soulful wisdom

---

Imagine a beautiful river, flowing downstream and startlingly clear. The day is crisp, the sun is shining, and the fish are swimming and enjoying life. Then, one day the river becomes polluted with oil and garbage. Once pure waters become dark and dirty, such that you can no longer see the light and it's hard to escape.

As children, we are bright, happy, and connected to our souls without fear and judgment. Then, one day something happens and we become traumatized. The trauma can stem either from a one-time event or be more complex, eventually resulting in a compounding of traumatic events that change us forever. Trauma can pollute our nervous system, and our brain, and dramatically change how we see the world. It is hard to see clearly from a wounded place, as well as to love, trust, forgive and live a happy and fulfilled life. Our bodies, brains and nervous systems can be seen symbolically as the polluted river. However, we are not always aware of this, nor of the impact this truth can have on our lives.

The concepts unveiled in this chapter will empower you with an understanding of how trauma impacts the brain and nervous system, as well as how to clear the pollution, heal from trauma, and take control of your life.

As a practicing Psychotherapist for over a decade and a half, I have learned that we cannot process trauma solely through cognition (as in talk therapy). As humans, we are souls and we are energy. When we combine the soul with science, we can generate healing and connect with our souls on a deeper level. This method combines energy healing, trauma healing, somatic processing, psychology and spirituality.

The problem I see, time and time again, is that people don't know what is happening in their bodies. When clients come to me for healing, they are often terrified. This chapter will help you understand how the brain is impacted by trauma, how the nervous system is affected (science), and how we can heal from within (soul).

A traumatic event is when a person is exposed to an actual or threatened death, serious injury, or sexual violence. The individual might directly experience the event, be a witness, learn about a trauma that has affected a family member or friend, or they may experience repeated or extreme exposure to aversive details of the traumatic event. For example, first responders and police officers are repeatedly exposed to crimes such as child abuse and often experience severe emotional, physical and psychological trauma as a result.

As we can see, there is a multitude of ways that trauma can impact people's lives, sometimes even unknowingly. Symptoms of trauma may include involuntary intrusive thoughts, nightmares, night terrors, dissociation, flashbacks, intense and prolonged physiological and psychological distress, and adverse reactions to internal and external cues. The consequences of trauma exposure can manifest in a variety of ways, including avoidance of people, places and situations that recall the trauma, self-imposed isolation, negative alterations in mood and cognition, distorted views of themselves, others and the world; feelings of detachment, hypervigilance, a proneness to being startled, lack of trust, problems with concentration, sleep disturbance, depersonalization and derealization.

These symptoms occur because of changes in the brain and the nervous system, impacting all areas of life, including relationships, family, health, and work.

What if you knew you could help yourself by learning about what is happening and reconnecting with your soul?

The Brain

When a person experiences trauma or is triggered, the amygdala identifies some form of threat stimuli and sends signals to other parts of the brain and nervous system, resulting in an automatic reaction known as fight, flight or freeze. This signal prepares the body for danger, in order to either deal with or escape the threat. The amygdala communicates with other parts of the brain, including the hypothalamus, which then releases cortisol. A person with PTSD may be triggered by anything the brain and nervous system consider a threat, even when there is no actual real threat. For example, if someone was in a car accident they may be afraid to drive again, or a child on a bike who falls off may then be afraid to get back on the bike. If the body believes there is a threat, there is a threat, and as Bessel Van Der Kolk states, "the body keeps the score".

The prefrontal cortex assesses threats and acts as a response system to bring the body back to a normal state. The prefrontal cortex is responsible for emotional regulation, impulsivity, decision-making, and interpreting emotions. When a danger signal is activated, the prefrontal cortex does not work effectively. This is where you may see yourself overreacting to a situation, as well as being triggered by a tone of voice, smell, situation, or any variety of possible triggers.

The hippocampus controls the brain's memory function and it is the place where files of memories are stored. After a traumatic event, the hippocampus might not code the event properly, particularly if it is an emotionally overwhelming event. Subsequently, one will have problems remembering aspects of the event, and the memory loss might even extend to everyday life.

Furthermore, neurotransmitters, or chemicals in the brain that regulate mood and other functions, can fluctuate in their levels. Imbalances in certain neurotransmitters, such as serotonin and norepinephrine, can contribute to an increase in symptoms, such as depression and anxiety.

The Nervous System

You can consider the nervous system like a river inside of our bodies. When the river is clean, the effects can be magical, but when polluted with trauma, many physical, emotional, psychological and medical issues can result.

The nervous system and brain are connected. When the brain is triggered to go into fight or flight mode, it sends signals to the nervous system to react appropriately. The sympathetic nervous system (SNS), and parasympathetic nervous system (PSNS), both play key roles in the connection with the brain and PTSD.

The SNS is responsible for the "flight or fight" response, and the PSNS is responsible for the rest and digest response.

When the SNS is overly activated, the sympathetic nervous system believes there is a real physical danger. This sends it into flight or flight, resulting in symptoms like anxiety, panic, panic attacks, rage, anger outbursts, hypervigilance, hyperactivity, rage, and overall intensified and out-of-proportion reactions.

When the PSNS is deregulated, the nervous system freezes as though there is a life-threatening situation. This can cause the person to actually freeze, collapse, and suffer from symptoms of depression, isolation, helplessness, collapse, exhaustion, numbness, and disconnection.

The beauty of this knowledge is that we can address symptoms with the awareness of what is actually going on in the body when the nervous system is seeking safety. Armed with understanding, we can effectively learn how to calm the river also known as our nervous system.

Immediate strategies to help regulate the nervous system

Imagine that your inner river is polluted and your goal is to clean it by practicing skills and techniques to rejuvenate and cleanse the water. Remember, you are in control and you are safe. I suggest implementing these strategies into your daily routine. Since the brain is conditioned in a certain way, and practice will help to change the patterns and conditioning over time, consistency is key. The more you practice, the more automatic a regulated response will become in a crisis situation.

Take 5 minutes for each exercise. You may do them for longer if you desire.

Step One: Grounding

Become aware of your surroundings, bring yourself into this present moment, and keep your eyes open. Grounding techniques help you center and anchor yourself into reality, and into this present moment. This is particularly helpful when experiencing flashbacks, anxiety and any dissociation symptoms.

Bring yourself to the present moment and take a look around you, what do you see, hear, smell, touch and taste?

What do you see around you? Voice your observations out loud, noticing colors, pictures, trees, people, and anything else in your surroundings.

What can you hear? Note sounds both inside and outside, such as birds, animals, or cars.

What can you smell? Burn a candle or essential oil that triggers a positive smell.

Touch the floor, a chair, or grass, or run your hands under water. Focus on how each experience feels, including the temperature and the sensation. Do this for a few minutes until you feel your nervous system calm down.

What do you taste? Taste something that is delicious to you.

Grounding brings you back to reality. When we are triggered, our bodies, brains and nervous systems believe we are actually back in the trauma. These systems do not know the difference between thought and reality, and so we need to practice techniques that let the self know that it is safe.

Step Two: Deep Breathing

Now we are going to work on calming the nervous system. Remember that when triggered, the heart rate increases and sensations of anxiety and panic all increase. However, two contrasting physiological states cannot exist at the same time. So when we control our breath, our SNS and PSNS will, by default, go back into a regulated state.

Take a breath; inhale for 4 seconds, hold it for 3 seconds and exhale for 4 seconds. Repeat this 20 times or more, as needed, until you feel that your nervous system is calm.

Remember, our nervous system cannot be in two states at the same time, so regulating your breath is a direct way to regulate everything else.

Now that you are calmer, the next step is to train your

brain to go into a state of safety.

Create a safe place in your mind and visualize yourself in this place of serenity or beauty. A unique location special to you may come to mind, or you might create one such as an ocean, forest, or lake. Be sure to pick a neutral place and not one that has any triggers associated with it.

Visualize yourself in this place, what do you see, hear, smell, touch and taste? Take a moment to truly absorb the beauty around you, in sight, sound, smell and feeling.

Notice your inner feelings, take a deep breath, and enhance these feelings. Now, take a few more minutes to really take in everything you see around you, as you connect with the emotion and the feeling of safety and calmness.

As you are doing this, identify a cue word that would remind you of this place, for example, maybe it is the word, "peace." Now say the word "peace" out loud 3 times, each time, closing your eyes, squeezing your fist tight, and breathing in that sense of safety, calm and peace.

Now identify how you feel at this moment. What are the qualities of this emotion? Has your nervous system calmed down? Let's keep going.

Step 3: Visualization

Take 10 deep breaths and on the inhale, visualize white or yellow light coming in through the crown of your head and flushing through your entire body. See a golden thread coming from Source through your crown and then down your body and into the ground, to the roots, grounding you from source to root.

Move your hands from your head to your feet, as if you are guiding the polluted energy through your body and out of your feet. When it is released from the feet, brush the energy away and let it flow into the Earth.

Do this 10 to 20 times. You may experience a range of emotions as you are releasing stored energy. Know that this is okay and that the energy is moving.'

Step 4: Butterfly Technique

Finally, implement the butterfly technique. This is an EMDR technique that uses bilateral stimulation, which triggers the parasympathetic nervous system to calm your nervous system, create a sense of peace, and decrease anxiety.

Place your hands like a butterfly and place them on your chest so each hand is underneath the shoulder blade.

You may keep your eyes open or closed, whatever you feel comfortable with. Focus on slowing down your breath and begin tapping as follows:

Simply tap the right hand, then the left, while focusing on your breathing. This is how you train your nervous system to gain control. After 10-15 sets (taps), take a deep breath and notice how you are feeling. Breathe into whatever comes up and begin to tap again. Know that you are safe and that you are in control.

Do 5-10 sets of tapping and breathing. When you are finished, note in your journal any thoughts, feelings and experiences that arise. Remember you are worth this time devoted to healing yourself, loving yourself, and growing and evolving into the life you have always wished for.

If you are interested in learning more tools to heal trauma please check out this resource;

The Eye Within The Soul; 9 Principles of Creating the Life You Desire. Sinead O' Hare, LCSW

Sinead O'Hare

Sinead O'Hare is a Licensed Clinical Social Worker/ Psychotherapist, EMDR Trauma Specialist and has been working in the trauma and mental health field for over a decade and a half. She is a Reiki Practitioner, and energy healer and has practiced using an integrated approach in her methods of treatment and healing.

Sinead's life experience growing up in Northern Ireland in the midst of what was called the 'Troubles', a Civil war experiencing intense violence and injustice, along with other traumatic life experiences, is what drove her passion for helping others who have experienced trauma. Sinead reports her mission in life is to serve others and help them heal from within and live the life they truly imagine.

Sinead has backpacked through Thailand, and Australia

and traveled to many other countries. Although born and raised in Northern Ireland, in her 20s, she relocated to America, pursuing her dream of becoming a therapist and author. She has worked with victims of crime, forensics and with individuals who have mental health issues and addictions, and who are involved in the criminal justice system. Sinead's mission is to help others achieve inner peace and happiness and to create greatness.

As a previous Chief Clinical Officer (CCO) of addiction and mental health treatment programs, she subsequently ventured out and is currently running her own private practice: Healing Within Counseling & Psychotherapy, PLLC, specializing in PTSD and trauma. Sinead uses a number of evidence-based practices, including EMDR therapy, to help those suffering from PTSD.

Contact:
Healing Within Counseling & Psychotherapy, PLLC
sineadohare@yahoo.com

PART 2

RELATIONSHIP TO EARTH, THE UNIVERSE, SPIRITUALITY, AND CREATIVITY

INCORPORATING ELEMENTAL LIVING TO RECONNECT WITH YOUR INNER FLOW: AN EXERCISE IN MOVING AWAY FROM ADRENALINE FUELED ACTION

by Kat O'Brien

Hustle culture relies on the push of adrenaline. It assumes that we are robotic and the same each day. This robotic forward push makes us rely on our adrenal glands and other stimulants, like caffeine & sugar. The hustle culture glamorizes lack of sleep and convinces us that self-care is a reward that we are only worthy of, once work is complete. This sets us up for burnout, and for anyone with a history of trauma, lays fertile ground for a freeze state to develop, as a result of overwhelm.

Living with the Elements recognizes that there is wisdom in nature, a wisdom that traditional cultures have aligned with for centuries. Living with the Elements is inspired by the cyclical pattern of nature. We know that every day need not look exactly the same, that each season has a different focus, and that no season is inherently neither good nor bad. Just as we would avoid planting a field in the dead of winter, or harvesting a crop just after planting, we can mold our modern lives to work with the natural cycles, versus against them.

An easy first step in reclaiming cyclical living is to acknowledge that each day of the week is actually named after a planet and that the planets have long since been tied to a specific element. Of course, living cyclically goes much deeper and can even be personalized for your unique soul blueprint. To begin, I will explain the connection of each day to the elements, which when harnessed, can be used to fuel us in a cyclical nature.

Monday - The Moon: the Element of Water

The Element of Water is traditionally linked to our emotions and spirituality. When we harness the power of water in our day, we create a day that is primarily focused on rest, emotional exploration, and spiritual practice.

While it may seem counterintuitive to start your week with a day of rest, there is great benefit in focusing your Monday on self-care. Putting yourself first is the foundation for a productive and sustainable week, in the following ways:

1. Filling your cup before filling others (family, clients, coworkers, creative projects). When we take care of ourselves, we have more to give to others.

2. Connecting into your Divine. When we begin our week with a focus on our spiritual connection, we can plan our tasks to truly connect to our higher purpose, versus the " shiny squirrel" tasks, the needs of others, or what society tells us to focus on.

3. Addressing Emotional Needs. Choosing to begin the week focused on our emotional needs and ensuring we can meet those needs, taking action to ensure they are being met, is another great way to ensure that our week is set up for success, by avoiding the risk of self-sabotaging emotions.

Great Activities to plan for Mondays:

- Begin the day with a longer meditation practice

- Begin your week with a quiet contemplation over a cup of ceremonial-grade cacao or herbal tea, and breathe your intentions into the liquid
- Reset your altar by adding new meaningful pieces, and your current intentions. Burn some incense and connect with your guides, angels and ancestors
- Pull oracle or tarot cards to help set intentions and directions, grounded in what is best for your highest good for the week
- Book a massage or other healing on Mondays, to rest and tend to your physical body
- Book your therapy sessions
- Bless your water with gratitude and your intentions for the week, and place a crystal of your choice on the water bottle
- Work with water element crystals - larimar, moonstone, opal, and malachite
- End your day with a bath

Tuesday - Mars: the Element of Fire

The element of fire is associated with our will and with taking action, movement, creativity and passion. When we harness the element of fire to fuel our Tuesday, we have a day focused on starting projects, moving projects forward, being creative, and getting our bodies moving.

Great Activities for Tuesdays:

- Plan your hardest workouts (lift heavy, go for that longest run etc.) for Tuesdays, to get that fire energy circulating throughout your body
- Get things started. Begin that creative project

that you have been putting off, don't worry about it being perfect, simply brainstorm and get the energy moving into a first draft

- Put on a great (upbeat, inspirational, even angry) playlist and dance. Move the energy of feelings throughout your body, to utilize energy stored as emotion.

- Tasks that are more solitary and focused in nature are great for Tuesdays, as you will be able to move in flow more easily. You are also likely to get more easily irritated with people who are "in the way" of your fiery creative energy

- Harness the power of fire by using your willpower to fast. You will likely be so inspired by your creative endeavors, that you won't even miss eating

- Look at the cards you pulled on Monday, and put their messages into action

- Work with fire element crystals - lapis lazuli, rhodochrosite, and sunstone.

Wednesday - Mercury: the Element of Air

Harnessing the power of the air element means that we prepare for a day of intellectual and mental pursuits, talking, short bursts of attention, and deep breathing. The element of air is associated with our mental body. Thus, air days are great for flexing our intelligent minds and our voices.

Great Activities for Wednesdays:

- Begin your day with a breathwork practice
- Schedule meetings, networking events,

collaborations, and client discovery calls. The element of air likes to talk, connect, and hear other opinions

- Bring the draft of what you created on Tuesdays to your team, for feedback
- Schedule your mastermind group and brainstorm solutions to challenges in moving your creation forward
- Do cursory research on items you need to build, on your fire day creation
- Learn a new skill
- Schedule your day to have short bursts of focus. Air days can make us scattered - so harness bursts of energy, by limiting activities to no more than 30 minutes throughout the day.
- Work with Crystals - aquamarine, azurite, celestite, and labradorite

Thursday - Jupiter: the Element of Earth

The element of Earth brings grounding, structure and stability to our lives. Earth days love systems, routines, discipline and a nice hearty 'to-do' list. The Earth element also loves nourishment and comfort. Ensure Earth element days are well-balanced between crossing things off your 'to-do' list and rewarding yourself for accomplishing so much!

Great Activities for Thursdays:

- Take everything you created on your *Fire* day, as well as the feedback you got from your peers, team, and co-creators on your *Air* day, and plug it into your system. Ensure that it comes to fruition and does not just remain a "good idea". Break it down into tasks that need completion. If you already did this on a previous Earth day, then begin work on your detailed steps

- Fine-tune the foundations of your business
- Streamline the systems for your business
- You will feel productive today, so take on that to-do list and cross bigger projects off the list
- Clean your house
- To keep that nourished, luxury-loving aspect of the Earth element happy, nourish yourself. Perhaps grab a delicious coffee and treat from your favorite coffee shop; pack a hearty lunch, make reservations with friends, family or your lover at a yummy restaurant, or simply grab takeout from your favorite place, and cuddle on the couch.
- Work with Earth Element Crystals - hematite, obsidian, pyrite, garnet, and tourmaline.

Friday - Venus: the Element of Water

The end of the traditional work week greets us with another water day. While the moon is more focused on our personal emotions, Venus is more focused on our relationships. Harnessing the power of the element of water in ways that involve our loved ones, is a great way to plan for this water day.

Great Activities for Fridays:

- Date Night - there is a reason that our culture has naturally seen Friday as date night, as it fits right into our need to connect spiritually and emotionally with our loved ones. However, we will likely feel more inwardly focused on a water day, so dates that are quiet in focus will feel most nourishing. Try a movie night, or candlelit dinner at home to talk about what went well in the week and how you can support each other going forward. Go for evening walks to share your dreams and aspirations, or enjoy a longer, deeper pleasure practice together

- Couples/Family Therapy - if you are in therapy with another human, harnessing the power of the water element on Fridays for group/couples therapy, can allow for an easier and deeper connection to your emotional needs

- If you are single, anything from Monday's list will be a great plan for Friday. However, incorporate an element of romance and love for yourself. For example, buy yourself flowers after work, journal on elements of a partner that you are looking to attract, take yourself out on a date, enjoy some oil added to your candlelit bath, or practice a solo pleasure practice.

Saturday - Saturn: the Element of Earth

Again we find ourselves harnessing the element of the Earth. Any activity from Tuesday can be repeated. Since our society considers Saturday a "normal weekend day", you might include any of the following:

- Make a meal plan for the coming week.
- Get to your local farmers market or farm stand and load up on local, fresh, and seasonal veggies, meats and eggs.
- Take some time to prepare meals for the week

(sensing a food theme for this Earth Element day?)

- Get your errands done for the week.
- Take time to set goals on a larger scale and plan your upcoming week.
- Finish the day off with a home-cooked meal around the table with those who ground you and represent family to you.

Sunday - The Sun: the Element of Fire

This is a day that anything from Tuesday can be repeated. You can also add in more of the Sun element by focusing on tasks that help you to personally shine! This is a GREAT day to PLAY!

- Move at your heart's pace today, have no schedule, do what lights you up and have fun

As you can see, when we harness the specific power of the elements on different days of the week, we naturally flow from rest to creation, to networking, and brainstorming, to eventually getting everything done. By working with the elements, we no longer need to rely on external sources to push us forward, because we are internally fueled.

Initial Activity

- Brainstorm all the things you do in a week and the outstanding tasks you still have to accomplish, both at home and at work
- Now go through the list and assign an element to the task by writing a W (Water), F (Fire), A (Air), or E (Earth) next to it
- Take out your calendar and schedule your

upcoming week, by placing tasks into the appropriate elemental day

- Keep your Master List to populate future weeks' planning

Maintenance

- Each Saturday, plan your week by doing a mini brainstorm or looking at your original master list and assign each task an element
- Schedule the task into the appropriate elemental day
- Implement and reclaim your natural energy flow!
- Notice how much calmer your nervous system feels after several weeks of operating in this natural flow

---

Kathryn O'Brien

Kathryn O'Brien (Hons BA Psych, Minor Religious Studies, MHSc Human Nutrition) is a former conventional nutritionist turned cyclic living advocate, stone medicine (crystal) practitioner, life transformation coach and ceremonialist.

Kathryn has worked with high-level elite athletes, new moms, women healing from extreme sexual trauma, entrepreneurs and people who are passionate about changing the world, who have found themselves lost and burnt out on their path.

Through her *Catalyzing Transformation through Connection Framework,* she leads people to create a more fulfilling life rooted in joy, nervous system regulation and trusting their intuition. The work is focused on three phases: Connecting IN with our physical body, Connecting OUT with our community and relationship with Nature and Connecting UP with our relationship to spirit/God/Goddess/Divine/Higher Self.

Kathryn currently resides in Guelph Ontario Canada with her teenage son. She is passionate about helping people remember their divinity and helping them create a life that brings them more joy and deeper connection

www.kathrynobrien.co
@katalyst_kat_

EARTH HARMONICS: GROUNDING INTO YOUR POWER

by Tyler Haubeck

What it does

This exercise shifts you into a state of grounded awareness, inviting and empowering you to access your own inner capacity to meet the stressors, edges, limits, pains, and triggers of life, and transmute them into expansive joyfulness. It is simple yet adaptable to any situation where you may find yourself feeling stuck, overwhelmed, or fearful. Breathe with the flow of life, tap into the powerful healing frequencies of Mother Earth, and move into a state of ease, calm, and focus, no matter where you are.

Who it's useful for

This practice is useful for anyone who struggles with anxiety, or often feels overwhelmed, or too stressed to function. It is also great for those who want a reliable way to tap into a flow state before work, exercise, performance, learning, etc. Those who struggle to generate clear, calm, grounded focus find this an effective way to catch themselves when feeling "out of it", crashing, and in need of an extra boost of clean energy. Above all, it is a powerful tool to meet challenging emotions, triggered states, or the edges of one's comfort zone with compassion.

Introduction

In my life as a human being, I have at times struggled to meet all sorts of stressors with my full awareness, intention, and capacity. I have run, hidden, and momentarily filled the void, creating patterns that helped make me feel better in the moment but didn't actually help me move through challenges effectively and enduringly. I eventually learned that we need to feel safe on a fundamental level in order to meet the challenges of life, and allow for a capacity to grow.

This is precisely the purpose of many grounding and meditation techniques in circulation, to help bring the individual to a state of calm, safety, home, and clear awareness so that they have a foundation upon which, to build the rest of their lives. This exercise is a remembrance of our own inherent abilities to find this place of home within ourselves, and offers a structure to integrate this state of consciousness with whatever life might ask of us. Whether it is used to feel deeper peace and mindfulness, to meet intense emotional triggers, to shift out of overwhelm and into focus, or to gently push through physical exertion, the magic of this practice lies in its adaptability and capacity to integrate it into the here and now, wherever that might be.

Grounding meditations are not new. Countless people from varied traditions practice some version of grounding. Personally, I never really "got" anything out of just sitting and trying to visualize the movement of my energy connecting with that of the Earth. I need more structure to move through the layers, unifying my awareness with the body, breath, and mind. I need to FEEL the vibrations on a physical level, to support my ability to shift into a state to do deeper work.

Once I was introduced to chanting, practices like grounding

started to click and work in a holistic way for me. When we chant LAM (the vibrational sound correlating to our root chakra), we are essentially vibrating our entire body into alignment with the Earth. Chanting itself, along with humming and singing, brings an embodied, active component to the grounding practice that is very supportive for helping the body fully relax, enabling deeper access to mindful states. Likewise, actively bringing our awareness to the body through practices like yoga or hiking, also helps connect our awareness to the expansive, supportive, abundant, and loving energy that is Mother Earth, who is waiting for us to commune and receive.

It was particularly through hiking that I began to adapt and integrate classic grounding techniques into an activity that is more "off the mat" and closer to the actions of daily life. I learned how to bring myself back home, to a place of safety and support wherever I am. Ultimately, I can tackle life genuinely feeling that the energy of the entire planet (and universe) is on my side.

I witnessed this truth in action when I was hiking the Grand Canyon rim-to-rim. Traversing 22 miles with over 10,000 feet in combined elevation change, along with carrying gear under the hot sun, was no walk in the park for me. I was forced - or, rather, intuitively guided - to come back to the breath and find rhythm and harmony between my body and the ground I walked upon. As I found a smooth rhythm with my step and my breath, I began to visualize my exhalations sending all my pain, exhaustion, and mental resistance down into the ground beneath me, to be absorbed by the Earth. I understood that Earth was eagerly open to receiving and composting these spent and stagnant energies. I knew I didn't need to carry them myself, and I felt supported and held on my journey. I actually felt immense physical relief, like receiving a massage, all my soreness and exhaustion melted away.

My breath became one with the cycle of the planet and expanded out to the solar system and beyond, to reach universal consciousness. Each new inhale came from the cosmos and through my crown, renewing and replenishing the energy I needed to keep climbing. Each exhale carried away all that didn't serve me, in my immediate goal to finish the 5,000-foot climb up to the north rim of the canyon. I felt ecstatic, euphoric, and beyond grateful. I also found myself pushing hard and making a great pace. My gratitude extended far beyond the experience of pain and suffering that might otherwise have been an easy point of focus. My experience was one of gratitude and nothing else; for all the pain and suffering, and for how challenging that hike was, I couldn't help but grin as each step was met not with resistance, but with grace.

Steps

Sitting comfortably or lying down, find a comfortable place where you can relax and express yourself freely.

Observe your breath as it is, noticing its flow, depth, and any tightness or restrictions.

Begin to take deeper breaths with greater intensity and purpose. Inhale through your nose, expanding first your belly and then your chest. Then exhale through your mouth and relax fully.

Pay attention to any tightness or disharmony in your breath and bring loving awareness to those areas.

Maintain this breathing pattern, focusing on purposeful inhalations and effortless exhalations.

If your breath feels tight or stuck, try to exhale audibly, sigh, tone, chant or hum to help relax your body and deepen your breath.

Scan your body with each exhale, consciously relaxing and releasing tension from the top of your head to the soles of your feet. You may even use your hands to intuitively massage your body.

Allow your body to move and express intuitively, following its natural impulses, knowing you are safe to do so.

Shift your awareness to the points where your body touches the Earth, feeling supported by the balance of gravity and the Earth's energy. Feel the way Mother Earth holds you, loves you, and supports you.

With each exhale, imagine your root chakra as a seed, sending your energy deeper into the Earth.

Chant the sound "LAM," "OM," or any intuitive expression to encourage your energy downward, vibrating through the diaphragm and out of the root chakra, guiding it down towards the Earth's core.

Spend as much time as you need here in this process of breathing, chanting, or otherwise vibrating your energy down into the core of the Earth, visualizing a great golden orb of light at the center.

When you have made contact with the Earth's core, feel and visualize yourself breathing in unison with this great light.

Then begin to draw this energy up with each inhale, visualizing this energy as a warm, golden light that travels up through your taproot, entering your body and filling it with vital, grounding energy.

As you inhale, feel this Earth energy spreading throughout your body, nourishing every cell and filling you with warmth, love, support, and a feeling of complete safety and relaxation.

Extend your exhale, settling into a deeply soothing rhythm as the Earth's energy settles and integrates into your entire being.

When you are ready, begin to imagine the energy expanding and radiating outward from your core, gradually extending beyond your physical body.

Allow yourself to feel deeply connected to the Earth, sensing support, stability, and unconditional love.

As you continue breathing, visualize yourself being firmly anchored to the Earth's core, like a strong tree with roots that penetrate deep into the ground and branches that reach towards the sky.

Invite yourself to feel and express gratitude for the Earth's nurturing energy, breathing in the exact medicine that you need in this moment, knowing that whatever you desire is already on its way.

Remain in this state of connection for as long as you desire, bringing the breath to its natural rhythm and allowing yourself to receive the love being transmitted to you.

Thank the Earth for its love and support and for composting any energy you may have released.

Tips for coaches to use with clients

Many individuals struggle to "get" anything out of most meditation techniques. A common explanation is that the body is too stressed for the mind to drop into the state of relaxation necessary for deeper meditation. Somatic practices, such as yoga or body scanning mindfulness practices, are very effective in helping the individual unwind before moving forward into the visualization portion of the practice. Toning and sighing also work wonderfully to activate the parasympathetic nervous system and smooth out the diaphragm, allowing for fuller and more connected breaths. When it comes to feeling into the root chakra and sending that energy down, I like to chant LAM to vibrate and activate the root, creating a physiological, vibrational component to the downward energy movement. Ideally, grounding practices are done outside in contact with the planet in some way, so that our bodies are supported by Earth's naturally grounding, electromagnetic flow. This practice has been described in an "on the mat" fashion, but the real magic comes in integrating this ability to feel grounded, safe, calm, and focused into our daily lives. In this way, we are empowered to meet challenges with loving awareness and feel supported by the immense, loving energy of the planet. Remember that you are not alone and that the unconditional support of Mother Earth is always available to you.

Tyler Haubeck

Tyler Haubeck is a Lifestyle Tuning Coach, who focuses on integrating lasting patterns into the lives of his clients. At the time of writing, he is completing his final training with Sacred Breath Academy, towards certification as a breathwork facilitator.

Tyler comes from a background of working within the mental health and education fields, where he has worked with a broad spectrum of individuals and focuses, including early childhood autism & behavioral therapy, teens and young adults with serious mental health disorders, and adults in serious psychological crises. He received his BA in Psychology from San Diego State University while contributing research in the scope of early childhood development. His experiences in the field, coupled with his personal mental health journey, have guided his ability to recognize and change patterns through achievable lifestyle practices, such as mindfulness, gratitude, movement, and breath - which Tyler finds offer the deepest insights and guidance towards becoming who he is meant to be.

Tyler spends time working in schools, competing in basketball, hiking, playing the guitar, singing, painting, creating herbal medicines, and traveling, all of which he considers training his capacity for mindful presence and creativity.

As Tyler moves into this new chapter and role as a breathwork facilitator, he is looking forward to working with individuals who are ready to tune into their higher selves - and breathe new life into their lives.

Instagram @bodymindunity

CREATIVE BITES: THE DANCE OF IDEAS, SKY, AND TRUST

by Iwona Fluda

August 31, 2023

Creativity, in all its facets and beauty, is not just a trait granted to a few lucky ones. It is also a human right, too often forgotten and frequently deemed unnecessary in a world where a mental approach to life has overridden all the beauty. Yet, tapping into our inner creative potential does not just bring much more joy into our existence; it also enlarges our experience of life beyond what we ever thought possible, fostering flourishing circumstances and revealing possibilities never imagined before. This is my invitation to you to discover your creative self. You can do so starting with Creative Bites, one bite at a time, and begin living your life to its creative fullest.

The idea of the following Creative Bite was one of those pestering seeds of creation that would not leave me alone, and believe me, I tried to ignore it. There are so many ideas out there, that I don't know how this one found me. It might have spotted me somewhere along the trail, during a summer hike in the Swiss Alps or after a long day's work, catching me while I sat back comfortably in my favorite chair, breathing in the fresh air deeply. Regardless of how and when they inhabit our minds, ideas are everywhere, almost floating in the ether. Ideas lie on my kitchen floor, scream from my wardrobe, chill between book pages, or silently await discovery in the trash bin full of unnecessary daily commitments. Wherever you find your ideas, the world becomes much more adventurous and quiet when you know that you can find them everywhere.

Today is not just about ideas, today is also about spaces. It is a common challenge to find a suitable space or create appropriate environments for ideas to flow into our lives across all aspects, including our relationships with our loved ones, as well as our other professional and private relationships. Fortunately, I found a way to enable the spark of inspiration to flow through and into the spaces we dwell in.

These are three golden rules:

1. Ideas. Every idea is a good idea - there is no such thing as a bad idea

2. Sky. Even the sky is not a limit - be wild with your ideas

3. Trust. Trust yourself and your intrinsic creative abilities - you know how to do this deep inside. And also, trust the people and process you're part of

Let us dive deeper into the three golden rules.

1. **IDEAS**: Too often, we are judged for our ideas, plans, ways of thinking, ways of living, the way we look, the way we speak, and the way we express ourselves. What if all of this doesn't matter because every idea is inherently good? An idea is good simply because it exists. Remember, precisely the way that every blank piece of paper is just a blank piece of paper, every idea is a good idea. It is what we do with our ideas that truly matters.

2. **SKY**: What if there are no limits? Imagine this for a

second. What if we agree that we can be as wild as we want to with our ideas in the time and space given to us? What if we leave all our insecurities, fears, and societal programming behind when we enter a room full of inspiration and possibilities? When it happens, my friend - everything changes at that moment.

3. **TRUST**: Nothing is more important than the trust created within yourself and the people and places around you. Our trust in the process, in the infinite possibilities of our minds, and in the world as a whole, allows us, not just individually, but also collectively, to discover countless opportunities and solutions for our lives.

When you enter a space where Ideas, Sky, and Trust rule, believe me, things will never be the same for you. Your world will shift into a space of infinite potential, and become a colorful playground.

These three golden rules for a space can be implemented everywhere. From our kitchen tables to our board rooms, they can make a significant difference in how we run our individual lives. This extends, in the end, to how we lead ourselves, and how we create our relationships, communities, and countries. Spaces where ideas thrive and can be explored and implemented, provide an immense feeling of endless possibility and can change everything.

Nevertheless, ideas are nothing without their implementation. Creative experimentation on any idea is precisely what it is named: an experiment. What I call the Creative Bites are small chunks of time where our creativity can flow. When you label your experiences, your next venture, and your following idea, a creative experiment, or a Creative Bite, you will not just take all the pressure off your shoulders, but also have much more space to play, experiment and have fun.

Here are a few 'Creative Bites' to indulge in:

1. Trust the paper - paper doesn't judge.

- Sit down for 8 minutes and write down ideas, responsibilities, and challenges for the next four weeks.
- Trust what you've written and set it aside until the next day.

Secrets behind this Creative Bite:

The constraints of time often push our creativity to the fore. When you're asked to write under a limited timeframe, a few things happen:

1. **Topic Anchoring**: Setting a specific topic or focus is like setting a destination for a ship. Even amidst the stormy waves of distractions and countless ideas, it provides a clear direction to sail towards.

2. **Intuitive Outpouring**: Under time constraints, your brain tends to bypass overthinking and the fear of judgment. It taps into the raw, intuitive parts of you, which offer some of the most authentic ideas.

3. **Brain and Belly Decluttering**: Yes, our gut is our second brain. And sometimes, we need to clear out both. Writing, especially the old-school way with paper and pen, acts like a sieve, filtering thoughts from both brains onto paper. It's a liberating exercise!

Personal Touchpoint: For many, like myself, this approach is not just an exercise but a lifeline during chaotic times. It's not just about writing, it's about finding clarity amidst the chaos.

2. Explore night-time musings.

- Write a pressing idea, or challenge, on a piece of paper
- Place the paper near your bed, e.g., stick it to the wall
- Upon waking, immediately write any new thoughts about that idea/challenge

Secrets behind this Creative Bite:

Sleep is when our brain is at its most creative. It is sorting, filtering, and connecting dots, without distractions of the waking world.

1. **Paper as a Confidant**: Writing down a challenge or a question is like sharing a burden. The paper doesn't judge or interrupt, it just receives.

2. **Mental Disengagement**: By offloading your thoughts, your conscious mind gets a break. Problems no longer need to be processed or solved immediately and sleep becomes an inviting respite.

3. **Subconscious Processing**: Your brain continues to work behind the scenes, untangling knots and finding solutions.

Personal Touchpoint: There's magic in entrusting the universe (or your subconscious) with your questions. The answers might surprise you in the morning! I shall not lie, I often find solutions this way.

3. Words have power - use them wisely and creatively.

- Monitor your speech for truthfulness, positivity, and value
- Only share if it's beneficial

Observe your feelings and emotions that arise when discussing positive versus negative issues

Secrets behind this Creative Bite:

Every word you utter is like casting a spell. Words have energy, vibration, and impact.

1. **Mindful Expression**: By being more conscious of our words, we understand their immense power in shaping perceptions and realities.
2. **The Power of Silence**: Sometimes, the most potent response is no response. Silence can be golden, allowing you to listen actively and absorb more.
3. **Energetic Resonance**: Words resonate beyond just their meanings. They influence energies, emotions, and even physical growth.

Personal Touchpoint: Understanding the weight of words can transform conversations, relationships, and our understanding of the world.

4. Become a sculpture - one emotion at a time.

- When you feel an emotion, make a sculpture with your body representing that feeling.

Secrets behind this Creative Bite:

Our bodies store emotions, sometimes more vividly than our minds. Embodying these feelings physically can lead to profound self-awareness and release.

1. **Embodied Awareness**: By turning emotions into physical postures, you become deeply attuned to how your body stores and releases feelings.

2. **Grounding Through Posture**: By embodying an emotion, you're essentially grounding yourself in the present, cutting through the mental chatter.

3. **Physical Release**: Letting go of the posture often signifies the release of the emotion, helping in emotional regulation.

4. **Rational Over Emotional**: This practice encourages a mindset where you start responding to situations with calm rationality, rather than impulsive emotion.

5. **Rediscovering Creativity**: Every posture and every embodiment is a work of art and a reminder of our inherent creative spirit.

Personal Touchpoint: Embracing emotions physically is not just an exercise; it's a dance of self-awareness, self-expression, and self-regulation.

Everything that comes out of creative experimentations, aka Creative Bites, can be defined as a success because you dared to make this happen by gifting yourself the time and space to play. This is especially true in the moment of transition when nothing is happening but everything is happening, when everything seems to be the same, but you have this constant feeling that nothing is the same, especially when nothing makes sense. When things fall apart and nothing seems to make sense, it allows us to create a space for creativity to flourish.

These days, the world needs audacious makers and doers who live beyond their societal programming and allow themselves to explore and play. As creativity is an innate human ability, imagine for a second how different our lives and the world would look, if we all gave ourselves a chance to tap into our intrinsic creative potential and live our lives in constant, creative awe. Imagine how differently we would make choices and dare to make necessary changes happen.

Today we have no choice but to live our lives creatively and show the world how we shine. The light is here to illuminate, and your creative intrinsic potential is that light. Allow yourself to shine brightly.

In your next pivotal moment of meeting someone new, entering a boardroom, beginning an important workshop or an important meeting, take a leap of faith and introduce people to the concepts of IDEAS, SKY, and TRUST, and let my magic unfold. Remember to dance with Ideas, Sky and Trust. Dance for the sheer joy of creation.

Iwona Fluda

Iwona Fluda stands at the forefront of creative thought, inspiring individuals and businesses to harness innovation, as the founder of the Ministry of Creativity LLC. Her dedication transcends mere occupation, manifesting as a profound commitment to nurturing creativity and instigating transformative shifts.

Her impressive educational credentials include two sets of Bachelor's and Master's degrees, complemented by her experience at MIT Bootcamps. Iwona's voice echoes on international stages, championing creativity in the digital age, and the integration of creativity with technology to catalyze business success. Her writings have graced Forbes DACH and her widely followed newsletter 'Creative Bites.' Iwona's expertise extends beyond entrepreneurship to the intricate dance of nurturing creative skills. and sparking significant change.

Iwona's expertise is also evident in her role as a designer and leader of creative workshops around the world, where she imparts her knowledge and ignites the creative spark among diverse audiences. As an RSA Fellow (The Royal Society for the Encouragement of Arts, Manufactures and Commerce), she is recognized for her work that seamlessly blends creative manual and cognitive thinking with practical application, emphasizing creativity as essential in leadership and organizational growth during the digital revolution. With her award-winning approach and global reach, Iwona Fluda is actively crafting the future of creativity in the business world and shaping the landscape of innovative leadership.

ON THE NATURE OF CREATIVITY: EXPANDING THE LANGUAGE OF PLAYFUL CONNECTIONS

by Rebekah Tolley-Georgiou

The 'What?'

The unexpected union between things that inform a language of creativity.

Pablo Picasso once said; *"Every child is an artist. The problem is how to remain an artist once he grows up"* (Davidson).

Over twenty years ago, I wrote a thesis for my Master's Degree in which I concluded, *"I believe I have reached the realization of myself as an artist working 'intuitively,' rather than one working in a purely formalized manner."*

Art can help us navigate our stresses and strains, and our triumphs and tragedies. It can dissolve borders or amplify divisions. Such is its power, it can also restore the sacred in a disillusioned world. Through the arts, we channel our values and our intentions, and we can offer spiritual meaning, perceptions and experiences across space and beyond time.

Instinct plays a central role in our development as artists and is a core essential quality of our very identity. By going within, by listening to our inner voice, and being 'playful', we may follow a path of instinctual turns. We then develop a greater sense of the self, and importantly, of self-trust.

The 'Why?'

By following the proverbial white rabbit down the self-trust hole, with practice, what we call 'hunches' can lead us towards an otherwise unexplored, expanding universe of thoughts and ideas (a stream of consciousness if you like). When harnessed, this may ultimately lead to new and greater forms of creative expression. Furthermore, it also allows us a renewal of intellectual and emotional opportunities. As we engage and evaluate our own cultural participation outside of ourselves, we learn how as artists/creatives we bring new knowledge and new perceptions to our own interpretations of the work of others. With consistent practice in following our instinct, our inner, innate voice becomes determinately refined, re-defined, and consistently evolving.

When we find ourselves excited by something, consciously and subconsciously we pour ourselves into it. We are at once stimulated intellectually, visually, and spiritually; and when our senses are elevated, we feel it in our bodies as a visceral, physical and emotional state of BEing, a mutual reinforcement - this is the frequency of things!

While we may not understand them, there is no denying our instinctual turns, often whispered or even shouted from within. We have an inkling to go to that place…speak to that person…or apply this color to that part of the canvas. As you lean into these instincts, they begin to pay off in ways otherwise unimagined. With practice comes self trust, which leads you to lean in even further, towards an ever more expanded universe, where new concepts and unfamiliar perceptions are waiting to collide with your imagination. As you begin to knit these together, the resulting fabric becomes, in summary, the creative self.

When we get fired up by anything, be it a topic, or a body of work (whether visual arts, literary arts, performing arts), it's almost impossible not to feel the palpable gathering of momentum, the confluence of disparate ideas, and the *what ifs?* This is the juiciest part of the experience, and opens up a path towards new ways of expression, where with focus and persistence, new concepts come bursting forth, offering previously unfamiliar insights and observations. This inner work drives the impulse and becomes a book, a film, a painting, a poem, a song... you can literally watch your own evolution unfold before you! The more you do this, the more you are 'compelled' to do this, and now you are lighting fires...big, beautiful, internal bonfires!

By BEing, doing, and thinking, your mind starts to enlarge and expand, creating never ending possibilities. You begin to see connections between things, regardless of how fragile and elusive they can often be. If you allow yourself to relax into a state of playful connectivity, or rather, 're-connectivity', watch how your perception suddenly takes off in other directions, and then allow for these new senses, hints, and intuitions, to further change, evolve, and shift. This is an organic process, so allow it to go where it will. The pay-off comes with consistent practice. The gift of a luminosity of thought, of impressions and ideas is, quite possibly like nothing else you will have experienced before. In turn, what you create from this 'center' will ultimately facilitate and energize the way that others - your audience - also visualize their world, both internally and externally. What opens doors for you, can open all sorts of doors, for other people. The internal declarations that create the works you make are made concrete in the world. As a result, the very spirit of 'play' helps others become better seers of their own world, the physical world, and all the realms beyond.

So, amplify that language of playful connections, discover unpredictable unions between things, gather that energy and create a piece of art, writing, a melody, a dance… BE PLAYFUL.

Let your instinct to create Art (in all its forms), be your spiritual escape hatch - meditative, transcendent, sublime.

So, let us dream of infinite, instinctive possibilities!

HINTS TO HELP EXPAND PLAYFUL CONNECTIONS:

- STAY CURIOUS. Einstein himself was quoted as saying that he had little in the way of exceptional talents, other than his passionate curiosity. His curiosity clearly got him quite far! Seek out playful connections between things and ask yourself, *"ok, so what happens if I do this?"*

- BE AWARE. *"There are two young fish swimming along and they happen to meet an older fish swimming the other way, who nods at them and says, 'Morning, boys. How's the water?' And the two young fish swim on for a bit, and then eventually one of them looks over at the other and goes, 'What the hell is water?"* (David Foster Wallace). So often we are blissfully unaware of the world around us, and the world within us. Take a moment. Meditate. Tibetan monks do it for hours! *This* is water.

- SEE THE FAMILIAR AS STRANGE. Salvador Dali certainly did just that. As he entered the theta brainwave state before falling asleep, he would 'download *'… vivid, irrational…images'* ' (David Gascoyne), often of everyday things - *hypnogocical images* as he called them. The meaning of these images remained a mystery, and indeed their interpretation was of little interest to him, but using them as a creative departure point, he was absolutely compelled to commit them to canvas. Perceive things not just how they are, but how they could be. Connect the seemingly unconnected.

- CHANGE YOUR HABITS. Humans are habitual thinkers and doers. Your 3D brain loves the familiar! Forming new habits, and stepping outside of your comfort zone, is the perfect breeding ground for creativity. Don't be afraid to be afraid! *"One doesn't discover new lands without consenting to lose sight of the shore for a very long time."* (André Gide).

- OBSERVE, DON'T WATCH. Tune into the world around you and the one within. Be present. Observe the work of others - not only those from your own area of creativity but equally as important, observe works from other disciplines. If you paint, read poetry. If you write music, study sculpture. *"A mind that is stretched by a new experience can never go back to its old dimensions."* (Oliver Wendell Holmes). Connections, connections!

- BE ADVENTUROUS AND OPEN-MINDED. *"Always go a little further into the water than you feel you're capable of being in. Go a little bit out of your depth. And when you don't feel that your feet are quite touching the bottom, you're just about in the right place to do something exciting."* (David Bowie). Remember, fortune favors the brave! This is where the magic happens.

- LEARN TO LISTEN TO YOUR INTUITION. By practicing deep, inner listening, you will create more space to receive tangible hunches, premonitions and inklings. The more we pay attention to these, the more we will encourage them to come forward. Remember, the word 'listen' is made up of the same letters as 'silent'...!

So where to begin:

Ask yourself the question*: 'What do I have an instinct about right now...?'*

Now, enjoy your journey down the rabbit hole!

Rebekah Tolley-Georgiou

Award-winning filmmaker, visual and sound artist, and educator

A graduate of EAVE (European Audio-Visual Entrepreneurs)

Location: United Kingdom

Website :www.rebekahtolleygeorgiou.art

Instagram: @rebekahtolleygeorgiou

Creative producer and co-author of the critically acclaimed feature documentary, *We Went to War*, a collaboration with the late Michael Grigsby, "...one of the giants of British documentary filmmaking" (BFI), which revisits a group of Vietnam War veterans, Grigsby first filmed in 1970, and which ponders the long term effects of war on both the individual and their families. Rebekah is also creative producer for award-winning *Okhwan's Mission Impossible*, a bicycle road movie about one man's pursuit of peace and a united Korea, executive produced by Academy Award winning director, Kevin Macdonald (*Touching the Void, The Last King of Scotland, The Mauritanian*); with elements from the film chosen for Ridley Scott's, *Life in a Day*.

Her documentary works have been award nominated at numerous international film festivals, with special screenings at the Museum of Modern Art (MoMA), New York, ICA London, and BAFTA Cymru, with video installation, sound works and visual art exhibited in the United Kingdom, South and East Asia, and the United States. She is a recipient of the Society of Scottish Artists, 125th (international) Annual Exhibition, Past Presidents Prize award, 2023.

As a University Lecturer at Postgraduate and Undergraduate levels, Rebekah has taught for many years in Art and Design, Contemporary Arts Practice, Experimental Film, Documentary Film and Global Cinema Narratives. She is a former lead moderator for undergraduate Theatre/Cinema courses and Fashion Design at Universities in Egypt and Pakistan. She continues to be on the jury panel for a number of national/international film festivals.

TRUSTING THE UNIVERSE: THE ULTIMATE LESSON

by Bethany Londyn

In my journey as an intuitive business and executive coach, I have come to understand that trust is the cornerstone of manifesting true success and fulfillment. Namely, fostering a deep belief that when you relinquish control and open yourself to possibilities, the Universe responds with a symphony of support, ultimately leading towards the realization of your dreams.

Great for people who:

- are frustrated about unaccomplished goals
- look to cultivate trust in the Universe, in order to open to all possibilities
- aim to release limiting beliefs and shift to a more positive mindset
- are business owners, entrepreneurs, and influencers wanting to align themselves with their desires

---

My clients, comprising business owners and CEOs, are driven by a relentless pursuit of results. Actually, let's be honest, it's me. I am the one who is obsessed with results, the one who is a spiritual *woo-woo,* who wants to meet KPIs for herself and for clients. I am the result addict, and the desire to succeed is ingrained in my DNA, as well as that of my clients. We approach goals with unwavering determination. However, in this fast-paced and result-centric world, there is a common thread that binds us - the need to control every aspect of our journey.

The desire for results is like a flame burning bright within. This fervent focus on outcomes, however, can lead to such a firm grip that the Universe's subtle orchestrations become constrained. It is as if the Universe, in its infinite wisdom, is ready to co-conspire and align the stars in a person's favor, but their tight grasp of control leaves little room for the magic to unfold.

Additionally, statistics reveal an intriguing insight into the human mind. On average, a person has about 60,000 thoughts per day, and astonishingly, most of these thoughts are negative and repetitive. This daily stream of negativity shapes our perception and influences our actions, often leading us to grasp for control, out of fear and doubt.

I have witnessed many business owners and individuals, not just in the professional world but also in personal life struggling with the need to control every detail… myself included. The subsequent pressure on oneself, on employees, and even on family, is stifling. This approach provokes a mindset of, "I must make this happen", and overlooks the gentle whispers of intuition and the guiding hand of the Universe.

Why this activation is important:

This exercise is a powerful antidote to patterns of negative thinking. It is designed to challenge limiting thoughts and create new neural pathways and synapses within our minds. By training your body, mind, and soul to embrace trust and surrender, you can liberate yourself from the relentless grip of control, and allow the Universe's divine orchestration to unfold in your life. The Universe is working tirelessly to co-conspire with you, aligning circumstances, people, and opportunities to bring about the very results you seek.

Through this activation exercise, you embark on a journey of transformation and an exploration of gratitude, surrender, and divine alignment. This ritual infuses you with the power of trust, creating space for the Universe to weave its tapestry of results.

In the face of 60,000 negative thoughts per day, rise with the determination to replace them with thoughts of trust, surrender, and gratitude. You will create new neural pathways and synapses that align with the divine forces that shape your destiny.

The benefits

This practice offers an array of positive outcomes that can enrich your life in numerous ways, such as:

1. Liberation from Control: Releasing the need to micromanage outcomes, allows you to flow with the natural rhythms of the Universe, bringing a newfound sense of freedom and ease.

2. Reduced Stress and Anxiety: The practice of challenging negative thoughts and embracing trust, leads to a decrease in stress and anxiety, causing the repetitive cycle of negativity to diminish.

3. Enhanced Intuition: Trusting the Universe allows you to tap into deeper insights and inner guidance, as well as ease in decision-making, for more efficient choices and outcomes.

4. Increased Resilience: Approaching difficulties with

a positive mindset and unwavering confidence in the Universe's support, empowers you to overcome fear and doubt, and therefore, face adversity with courage and determination.

5. Enhanced Relationships: This exercise transforms your energy, making you more approachable and compassionate, enriching both personal and professional relationships.

6. Greater Alignment with Goals: By training your mind to focus on trust and positive possibilities, you align yourself more closely with your goals, releasing limiting beliefs and opening the door to a world of new opportunities, previously obscured by negative thinking.

7. Manifestation of Desires: Cultivating trust in the Universe's benevolence turns you into a powerful magnet for manifestation, elevating your frequency with positivity, allowing you to attract opportunities and experiences, aligned with your goals and desires.

8. Inner Peace: Trusting the Universe brings deep inner peace and contentment. As you find solace in the support of a higher power, serenity permeates throughout all aspects of your life.

9. Transformational Growth and Improved Mental Well-Being: The exercise of challenging negative thoughts and embracing trust, catalyzes personal growth and transformation. This inspires you to step out of your comfort zone, face fears, and embrace change with grace and optimism.

Your New Evening Ritual:

Welcome to this transformative exercise, designed to challenge the status quo of negative thinking, and embrace the boundless possibilities that result from trusting the Universe with unwavering faith. By surrendering to the flow of life, you discover your true essence and find fulfillment in both your professional and personal endeavors.

I know this because of the consistent magic I have been witnessing, surrendering to, and receiving. I will share more about this in my story below.

This crafted activation exercise is intentionally simple yet potent, inspired by my experience with clients who achieve great gains from small tweaks. I have witnessed how subtle shifts in perspective and daily practices lead to profound transformations. Infuse your mind, body, and soul with the energy of trust, and you create space for the magic of manifestation to unfold.

1. Think about your goals and desires. It could be weekly, monthly, or yearly goals. Even if the goal is simply to feel more peace in your life, this is a noteworthy goal.

2. Dive into a journal. Take inventory of your day and write down "*10+ Ways the Universe Has My Back*". You want to prove to your 3D mind that your goals are in line and happening, which will in turn open you to receiving even more support and synchrony. Examples could be seemingly small gestures, such as finding a much-needed parking spot, receiving an unexpected message from a friend, or signs guiding a decision. These simple acts of support are often the Universe's way of saying, "I am here with you, your achieved goals are en route."

3. Make it a nightly ritual. Shift your focus from challenges and setbacks to moments of support, guidance, and synchronicity that occurred throughout the day. Rather than dwelling on what went wrong, you start to deliberately seek out instances where the Universe has your goals supported.

Unlike a conventional gratitude list, where you might enumerate what you are thankful for, this exercise prompts you to recognize the subtle yet profound ways the Universe co-conspires with us. It invites you to seek out the hidden gems of support and synchronicity. By training your minds to seek out these moments of support and synchronicity, you are creating new neural pathways and synapses that challenge the grip of negative thinking.

After following this practice for even a short time, you will notice a shift in your mindset. The focus on trust and gratitude starts to overshadow the persistent negativity that once dominated your thoughts. The daily repetition of this exercise strengthens the neural connections associated with positive thinking, anchoring us in a state of receptivity to the Universe's blessings.

Through this simple exercise, you learn the art of surrender, which is to release the need for control and instead allow the Universe to lead the way. You discover that the real power lies not in relentless control, but in the profound trust that everything is coming together for your highest good.

My Experience:

Shifting my focus from a gratitude list to recognizing how the Universe supports my goals, was extraordinary. The first night, as I wrote "10+ Ways the Universe Has My Back," excitement and gratitude surged within me. I noticed subtle signs of support, like how a session cancellation (which was initially frustrating), allowed me to get caught up on something else that was important.

The next morning, I felt lighter with a newfound ease and flow. My trust deepened, guiding me through challenges with optimism. The exercise rewired my mindset in one evening, aligning me with possibilities and strengthening my intuition! The shifts were profound, and I noticed my mind racing to find the next sign of a benevolent Universe supporting my goals. The practice deepened my connection and appreciation of trusting in the Universe.

Even this week as I finalized this piece for the book, I lost my keys. While this could be a huge frustration, the magical result is that through losing my keys, I connected with multiple people out and about in my neighborhood.

Losing the keys has opened doors and is yet another example of the Universe having my back! Two of these people are business owners that I may collaborate with, and we might never have met had I not lost my keys.

This trust-activating exercise is continuously transforming my own life and those of my clients. I am seeped in stories of increased serendipitous opportunity, improved relationships, and enhanced decision-making that arises from this practice. By releasing the need for excessive control and finally embracing trust, people experience newfound ease in navigating challenges and bringing about epic results.

Trusting the Universe's support opens doors to possibilities and ignites flow and guidance. This powerful tool conquers trust, one of the biggest lessons for a human, leading to breakthroughs and magical results.

Grateful:

I am excited to learn about how this powerful and simple activation creates new experiences that align you with the magic of the results. Let's open ourselves to infinite possibilities and invite the grace of the Universe to unfold in our lives like never before.

Bethany London

Bethany Londyn is a globally celebrated Intuitive Revenue Strategist and Transformational Coach, known for her innovative blend of intuitive wisdom and strategic business insights. With a client list that spans esteemed companies and high-profile leaders across the United States, Bethany is also a respected contributor to platforms like ThriveGlobal, YogaJournal, and MindBodyGreen.

As the visionary behind Londyn Heights, Bethany leverages her intuitive skills to unearth hidden opportunities and potential challenges, offering her clients not just strategic advice but also energetic healing. She is the trusted strategist for CEOs, Business Owners, and Influencers, who are committed to achieving both personal fulfillment and financial prosperity.

Often referred to as the 'Billionaire Catalyst Coach,'

Bethany has an impressive track record of driving revenue growth. Among her notable achievements is doubling a company's sales from $8 million to $16 million in a mere two months—a feat she has consistently replicated for various businesses.

Her latest best-selling book, "Get Aligned Now," serves as an empowering guide for those looking to tap into their inner wisdom. The book has been praised as a transformative tool that enables readers to reach unprecedented levels of high performance and tangible results.

BethanyLondyn.com
LondynHeights.com

PART 3

RELATIONSHIP TO THE QUANTUM
AND ENERGETIC MODALITIES

QUANTUM SOUL ACTIVATION: A METAPHYSICAL APPROACH TO HUMAN EVOLUTION

by Lauren Dickinson

This Technique Is for You if:

- You are a high performer looking to optimize your health and performance
- You want to elevate your consciousness and reprogram your brain
- You want to deepen your spiritual practice and become immune to stress
- You want to discover and activate your soul's purpose

A Background of Stress: The Zeitgeist of Our Modern Culture

Despite modern luxuries and conveniences, achieving inner peace is increasingly elusive in our fast-paced world. External stressors, including our high-tech culture and environmental toxins in our air, water, and the food we consume, all precariously impact our bodies, minds, and spirits.

Dr. Hans Selye, known as the father of stress research, postulated that "It is not stress that kills us, but our reaction to it." He introduced stress's medical context and revolutionized our understanding of disease. In his 'General Adaptation Syndrome' theory, he defined stress as the source cause for all manifestations of disease.

The Devastating Effects of Stress on the Brain

Humans are a vibrational system, operating in a vibrational frequency universe. Since the brain doesn't know the difference between a real or perceived threat, it uses its energy for survival rather than directing energy for healing. In an inappropriate stress state (such as focusing on a perceived but not real threat), brain waves lock into *beta* waves, with very few *alpha* waves. Being in an *alpha* state is the gateway to our subconscious mind and lies at the base of our conscious awareness. The voice of *alpha* is our intuition, and these waves are also required for healing and regeneration. In a chronic stress state, our brains lateralize and lock into hemispherical imbalance, with heightened *beta* waves on one side and minimal activity on the opposite side. This can all be measured and demonstrated visually on EEG scans.

When our brain lateralizes during the stress response, this causes excessive muscle tension on the opposite side of the body that it controls, with excessive weakness on the other side of the body. This can be measured with a simple kinesiology test. With overly excessive tension on one side of the body and excessive weakness on the other, this imbalance leads to spinal stress areas and biomechanical distortions, as the hips pull up and the spine contorts in an "S" shape.

Structural Distortion and Life Force Energy

When our structure is altered, function follows. All cells in the body must have a high amount of voltage in order to repair themselves. Structural imbalance affects our Cerebral Spinal Fluid, which is a **luminous** fluid that carries Life Force Energy, coming from the brain through the spine. With it comes vital information from the brain and even downloaded programs from our thoughts and emotions, which travel through the spinal cord and out our nerves. In areas of structural distortion, the body is not getting the life force it needs in order to regenerate and heal. Chiropractors call a spinal stress area a "subluxation."

104

Interestingly, if you break down the word from its Latin roots, you get **sub**: less than; **lux**: light, and **ation**: state of being. So a spinal stress area, or a subluxation, literally means a state of being less than light.

In Einsteinian physics, we understand that all matter is energy vibrating at different levels of frequency, and the difference between physical matter and subtle energy matter is only its frequency. The human system as a multidimensional energy system has its beginnings in what is called the causal body, which is pure spirit or soul in esoteric anatomy and spirituality. From there, we vibrationally step down in creation and matter, through denser manifestations of energy into the mental body, astral/emotional body, etheric body, and finally the physical body. If we can understand disease and health as a priority system of above-down and inside-out, we would be far better at stymying the progression of chronic, degenerative and debilitating diseases. In the alternative medicine paradigm regarding subtle energy, life force is the causal agent behind healing. When there is stress, there is a diminished flow of life force. Where there is little light, there is little healing. Addressing the physical manifestations of disease, as in the Western medicine paradigm, is only addressing the symptoms of disease, not the cause. If there is to be a radical shift in the way we collectively heal, we must have a radical shift in the healing paradigm on an individual level. Western medicine by its very genesis will never offer true and lasting healing.

Seven Levels of Brain Function and the Implications of Unrelieved Stress

Physiologists tell us that there are seven levels of brain function. In an evolutionary sense, when a higher level of brain activity comes into being, the wisdom within doesn't discard the old and keep the new, but instead, it encapsulates the old with the new. As we have evolved, so too have our brains. For today's purposes, we are going to focus on this reptilian brain, the mammalian brain, and the human brain, and why they matter in the context of whole brain functioning.

The **reptilian** brain is also known as the limbic system. Its purpose is fundamentally that of the physical survival of the body. In times of perceived danger, the flight or fight response is activated, and all energy is focused on the survival of the organism.

The **mammalian** brain gives us a sense of care and concern for others, and it has a great deal of warmth. It is the source of our humanity and human feelings. Like the reptilian brain, it operates primarily on a subconscious level.

The **neocortex, or the human brain,** is the outer and seventh layer of brain tissue that overlays the surface of the two hemispheres of the brain. There is a tremendous amount of research demonstrating that the integrated seventh brain is the highest level of brain function. It is present in all primates, but most developed in the human brain.

The neocortex is the spiritual brain that is nourished by love, peace, and balance. It is the part of us that is in tune with the infinite. When we are in a unified state, a state of balance, wholeness, and harmony, this human brain is in control and our Higher Self runs the show. Unlike the other brains, the human brain operates on a mostly conscious level.

In times of danger, or perceived danger, energy must move into the lower levels of the brain for survival. In the fight or flight stress response, we are in a lateralized, lower level of brain function with corresponding biomechanical weakness and tension. Life is lived at half-mast; the more we stay in lower brain levels, the more chaos we have in our lives. **Our spiritual growth depends on our ability to stay mostly in our human brain.**

If you are familiar with the concept of neuroplasticity, you know that our neural pathways are created and sustained by the dominant thoughts, beliefs, behavioral patterns, and emotional states of being we find ourselves in consistently. This means that when we are stuck in our reptilian brain, we cannot access our latent spiritual potential until we break this pattern and reprogram the brain.

When our brains become balanced, we are no longer locked in the *beta* survival state, and we become free from societal programming and constraints. We become sovereign, autonomous beings. We deal with stress effectively, we form our own thoughts, and we make our own decisions; free even from the matrix programming and opinions of our peers. With this inner freedom, our potential to love, create, and grow spiritually is wonderfully magnified and we have the power to transform our lives.

As we heal ourselves as individuals, and express empathy for the human condition we all share, our ability to spread healing on a vibrational level is exponential. This is just a fraction of the true potential of energy medicine, and acts as a compass to actualize and live our human potential in this lifetime. In universal terms, and not exclusive to one religion, culture, or belief system, we were born in the image and likeness of our creator; whether we call it source energy, God/Goddess, or the Universe. The truth is that we are here to create, with just as much love, joy, and abundance with which the creator created us. Our soul's purpose is uniquely tethered to the things that we love and feel inspired to create, as an expression of the creator's own brushstroke. This begs the ultimate question: what are we capable of when our brains are in balance, when we are inner-actualized, and when we create at our highest potential?

A Light Body Activation for Higher Consciousness

Although there are a number of energetic healing modalities that can help balance and reprogram the brain, my preference is a method we can do ourselves to drop into *alpha* brain waves almost instantly. With continued practice of this technique, we reduce our dependence on outside 'healers' and empower ourselves to take charge of our own healing. This meditation is a technique I developed, while working with clients to open the energetic gateways of their innate wisdom and self-healing. When we are in the *alpha* state, this is the best time to reprogram the brain and create new neural pathways. When we do this exercise while we are already in the balanced *alpha* state, we prolong this state of being, and further increase our ability to sustain a *new way* of being.

1. Sit comfortably in an upright position while keeping your spine straight and hips grounded evenly into your seat. Close your eyes and begin with slow and deep breaths, feeling your breath slowly filling your chest cavity before you exhale.

2. As you bring your attention to your slow and relaxed breath, imagine a small white orb in your mind's eye, just in front of your closed eye gaze. Take a few breaths while imagining this orb floating in front of you.

3. As you take your next inhalation, imagine that white orb entering your forehead at the third eye point between your eyebrows. Exhale slowly and feel it enter further into your headspace. With each effortless inhalation, imagine the white orb being breathed into the very center of your brain, between the two brain hemispheres, where your pineal gland resides.

4. Imagine the white orb expanding outward to the edges of your cranium. With each breath, visualize the white light gently pulsing outward from your pineal gland,

now activating your crown chakra from the inside out.

5. Begin imagining this white and luminous light slowly and gently traveling down to the base of your skull, where your brain stem lies. Imagine the light gently pulsing and activating your brain stem from the inside out. Take a number of gentle breaths as you feel your head filled with this luminous orb, that has now become your waking consciousness.

6. Slowly begin to move this luminous energy down your spine. First, it lights up your neck as your muscles begin to relax. Feel it gently warm your throat chakra in the front and continue down through your upper thoracic area. Feel your heart expand in gentle, blossoming petals, as the luminous energy flows down your spine and feel your muscles relax and unwind.

7. With each inhalation and exhalation, the white light gently flows further down your spine, activating and awakening your solar plexus chakra, your sacral chakra, and your root chakra, as your lower body and extremities gently warm and pulsate with luminous energy. As the white light reaches the base of your spine, imagine that your entire body is now filled with this luminous energy, gently radiating outward from your being and filling the room around you. Continue breathing as the light expands into the whole space you occupy; then traveling outward to the entire neighborhood, city, and State. With every breath, gently and slowly imagine this white light expanding across the continent and enveloping the planet, galaxy, stars, and the totality of the universe itself until it reaches its source point. Try this out on yourself and teach it to your clients who want to deeply and truly activate their lives.

Lauren Dickinson

Artist, Shamanic Energy Medicine Practitioner, Quantum Shamanic Soul Coach, Founder of Orion Retreats

Lauren knew at an early age that she wanted to help people in the form of energetic, hands-on healing. She started her formal studies in coaching and energy healing as a young adult, leading to a life-long pursuit and quest to facilitate soulful healing and its highest expression for her clients. Her studies have included professional certification and studies in Core Synchronism, Reiki as a Master Practitioner, Alphabiotics, professional coach training, metaphysical studies, bioenergetics, Shamanism, and most recently, the Enneagram.

With a well-rounded and practical knowledge base in a wide variety of applications, Lauren loves to co-actively facilitate a greater expression of life energy, healing, and personal awareness and growth for her clients. She is deeply drawn to sacred energy centers of the earth, most notably having lived in Sedona, Arizona and spending time with an Aboriginal tribe in Uluru, Australia. She currently lives in Mount Shasta, California, considered the root chakra of the world.

Lauren is the founder and CEO of Orion Retreats. Orion Retreats is a curiously innovative collective of inspired creators, thought leaders, and wellness warriors who create bespoke retreats that enliven the spirit and empower guests to live their lives on purpose. Each retreat is uniquely designed at powerful sacred energetic points on the earth, to help guests awaken to their divinity and create the life of their own design, as only their soul can envision it. To learn more, please visit our gallery of retreats and facilitators at www.orionretreats.com.

Lauren is also an international, award-winning visionary multimedia artist and teaches artists and non-artists alike how to tap into their innate creativity and birth their creative genius into the world.

Please visit www.orionretreats.com/aylbonus

FEELING ENERGY: A METHOD OF BODY SCANNING YOUR ANIMAL COMPANION

by Laura Kilmer

Everything is made up of energy. A perfect example of being able to see energy is when you see heat waves rising from asphalt on a hot, sunny day. Most people have seen this, but have you ever tried seeing energy in an inanimate object? You can experiment with this phenomenon using your phone camera. Set the camera to video (but don't press the record button), and lay it flat (with the camera facing down) on any hard surface, with the end closest to the camera lens propped up about 3mm, just enough to allow a small amount of light to come through. You will see the energy of the surface below your camera vibrating in pixels on your screen.

Feeling energy is just as simple as seeing it. Once you learn what energy feels like, you can take it a step further by doing a body scan on your animal companion, another human, or any other living thing.

Great for:

- Anyone who is concerned that something might be wrong with their pet
- Anyone who wants to find energy blocks or disturbances in their own body
- Anyone who wants to learn how to feel energy and foster deeper relationships, and sensitivity to others

Throughout my studies, I have learned many forms of body scanning and energy healing, including Reiki, Crystal Healing, Pendulum Dowsing, and Chakra Clearing. I have also studied lesser-known techniques, such as becoming one with another physical body, using clairsentient communication to share feelings and emotions, and a method referred to as "Healing Hands", where you can learn to feel the energy in the auric field of your animal companion. Today, we will begin with a simple exercise in learning to feel energy in your hands, followed by a technique to conduct a body scan on your pet.

FEEL YOUR OWN ENERGY

To begin, ground yourself. There are many grounding methods taught on numerous platforms, so it's a good idea to try various techniques until you find what works best for you. The method I like to use is to sit comfortably with my eyes closed and feet on the floor. I begin relaxing by taking slow deep breaths and holding them in, before very slowly releasing the breath. After I have become quite relaxed, I visualize a white energy cord extending down from above and entering my body from the top of my head. This energy flows down through my body, exits my feet, and continues down into the ground, where I visualize it wrapping itself around a large garnet crystal, in a cavern at the center of the Earth. This energy then flows back up through the ground, enters my feet, travels upward through my body, and exits the top of my head. As a result, there is a continuous flow of energy connecting me from above and below, as it travels in both directions through my body.

Now, stand with your feet shoulder-width apart. Rub your palms together vigorously for 15-20 seconds, feeling the heat build-up between your hands, then stop and slowly pull your hands away from each other to about 1 inch. Pay attention to the sensations in your hands, as well as what is happening between your hands. You may feel tingling, warmth, or a sensation of electricity flowing back and forth.

Now slowly pull your hands about 6 inches apart, and then bring them back together without touching your palms. As you slowly go back and forth, you will feel a sort of magnetic pull as your hands get further apart, and then the energy will begin to feel heavy and solid as you push them back together. This is your energy, your Life Force. You cannot see it, but you can feel it. It is real and it is tangible.

As you play with energy, you can bring your hands further apart and then back together again, never touching your palms. If your connection is still strong, rotate your hands so they are above and below rather than side to side – this is your energy ball. Push your hands in and out, up and down...play with it!

If you lose connection, simply begin again by rubbing your palms together. If you play with this every day, you will soon be able to keep the energetic connection, while spreading your hands really wide.

EXERCISE:

Practice this technique in a dimly lit area with a dark surface behind your hands. When you are pulling the energy back and forth, change from your hands to using only your index fingertips. As you slowly pull your fingertips apart, you will see the energy running between your two fingertips. Now you can see that the energy is real.

BODY SCANNING:

Every living being has an energy field. Although invisible to most people, this bubble of energy envelops the physical body as well as running through it, supporting the body's very existence. This energy field is referred to as the *aura*, which consists of several layers and connects to the physical body of the person/animal, via energy centers, called chakras. Within this framework, everything is recorded energetically. Each time there is physical or emotional trauma, it is recorded in the energy field. With time, these traumas build up in the energy field and can create blockages to the body's natural energy flow, resulting in "dis-ease" either physically, mentally, emotionally, or spiritually.

Using your hands to conduct a body scan as a method, can be used both from a distance, as well as in physical proximity to your subject.

It is important that you check yourself physically and emotionally before beginning a body scan. It is essential that you can distinguish your own ailments from any ailments of the animal you are body scanning. Take a deep breath and set the intention that you are relaxing your body. On each exhalation, allow your body to relax more and more deeply, becoming aware of any tension, anxiety, fear, worry, or stress you may be holding, and release it on each out-breath. After you are relaxed, begin at the top of your head and mentally scan every single part of your body, becoming aware of any pain or tension you may be experiencing. Write any findings down immediately. Not only will this act as a guide to what sensations belong to you in your energy scanning work, but it will also serve as an action plan for meeting your body's identified needs, whether physical, emotional, or spiritual. Give yourself permission to support your own healing, before rushing into a body scan of another. It's important that you work on the issues that have arisen for you. The clearer your own energetic body, the better your body scanning results will be when you work with animals.

BODY SCANNING ANIMALS:

Begin by grounding yourself and warming your hands up as practiced earlier. Then set your intentions and connect with the animal that you will be scanning. To create your own intention and connect with your pet may be as simple as "It is my intention that I can easily feel the energy of _____, and that any disturbance I feel will be coming from _____, and not from me."; Create whatever sounds best for you as you set your own intention.

To conduct the body scan, I find it easiest to use a teddy bear as a surrogate for the animal, however, many people simply close their eyes and visualize the animal standing in front of them. Find what works best for you and use that technique during your scans.

Begin by placing your hands at the nose, and then very slowly and purposefully, bring your hands down the sides of the head, paying close attention to any changes in the feeling under your hands. You are working with the animal's energetic field, so if using a surrogate, keep your hands up off the surface of the teddy bear. If visualizing your companion, move your hands over the image in your mind. Bring your hands over the head, down the neck, over the shoulders, and down the back to the tip of the tail. As you slowly move your hands over the animal's energetic body, notice how your hands feel. Did you feel any changes in energy? Was there a difference in what you feel under your right hand compared to your left? Did you feel hot or cold spots, tingling, an emptiness, or maybe you even had a sense of the energy being stuck or blocked in areas? Make note of where you felt any sort of disturbance.

When you reach the tail, continue in a sweeping motion and flick the energy down into the ground, with the intention that it is returned to the universe to be cleansed and recycled.

Bring your hands back to the left shoulder, and move them slowly down the leg to the foot/hoof, paying close attention to any changes in energy sensation, or flow. Flick the energy down into the ground as before, and make note of any perceived disturbances.

Repeat this technique with the right front leg, then take your hands to the left hip area and slowly scan down the left back leg. Repeat on the right back leg, again making note of any disturbances felt.

Finally, begin back at the nose and slowly scan under the chin, down the underside of the neck, across the chest, down between the front legs, and underneath the animal to the tail, flicking the energy into the ground and making note of any disturbances.

When you are finished scanning the body, energetically disconnect with your animal friend by shaking your hands and stating the intention that you have completed the scan and are now disconnected.

How did that feel for you? If this is new to you and you are unsure of what you are picking up, remember that this method requires a certain level of energy sensitivity on your part, so you may wish to continue to practice feeling your own energy, and then return to the body scanning later.

It is important to note that everyone CAN do this. We were all born with this ability, but most of us have forgotten how to use some of our more obscure senses as we age. Feeling energy does not require a psychic sense or special gift. Perceiving energy also does not interfere with any religious belief, and can easily be learned by anyone with practice.

BODY SCANNING IS NOT A SUBSTITUTE FOR VETERINARY CARE**

You are scanning to detect disturbances in **areas** of the body, not specific organs, bones, muscles, or other internal body parts. It can, however, aid your vet in their diagnosis as you share the information from your scan.

- While you are learning the body scanning technique and building your confidence, I recommend you work with animals that you are not worried or fretful about. This allows you to focus without pressure, and remain objective and impartial, as the feelings and sensations are felt in your hands.

This same technique can be done on any living being. It can be helpful to practice with family and friends, so they can provide you with feedback.

Always keep in mind that any energy disturbance or block you feel doesn't always mean a physical ailment is present. Many blocks and disturbances are emotional, mental, or spiritual. Most vets are not attuned to these subtle senses. Body scanning is a valuable tool. A felt disturbance in your body scan can guide your vet in ruling out physical conditions. Subsequently, it can be useful to enroll other experts, such as an animal chiropractor, holistic vet, or even an energy healer, to clear any emotion or trauma that may be creating the block.

As you learn to feel your own life force energy, the most important thing is to have fun with it. Next, you can learn how to feel energetic disturbances in any body that you are scanning, thus deepening your connection and relationship to everyone around you.

Laura Kilmer

Intuitive Animal Communicator, Reiki Master and Energy Healer
Website: www.animalchats.net
Email: ltkilmer@gmail.com and laura@animalchats.net
Location: Springbrook, Wisconsin, USA

Laura is a Professional Animal Communicator, Reiki Master, Animal Reiki Practitioner, Crystal Energy Healer, Pendulum Dowser, Chakra Energy Balancer, Essential Oil Practitioner, and a lifetime student in Universal Energy and different Healing Modalities, especially those pertaining to animals. Laura has also studied Canine and Feline Nutrition since 2014, and currently feeds her dog and four cats nutritionally balanced and species-appropriate diets.

Laura grew up on a farm with a large variety of animals and in a family with 5 other siblings. Although there were many human members in the home, she preferred to spend a lot of her time with the various animals on the farm, even recalling an event when she was approximately 11 years old, when she ran away from home with her horse and dog, but returned home a few hours later after the two animals convinced her that it was the right thing to do (her mom knew where she was the entire time). As she got older, she continued to talk with animals, but had been told by so many people that it was just her imagination, that animals did not talk to humans, so she slowly closed off her innate telepathic communications, despite remaining very close to sentient creatures throughout the majority of her life, and never living without at least one animal companion in the home.

Laura is a Reiki Master, having learned many different energy healing modalities and techniques, and reawakening her telepathic abilities to communicate with animals. She has studied under many different animal communicators over the years, and has recently become a Professional animal communicator herself.

During the Pandemic in 2020, she began working at a Human Society, where she was able to begin helping animals. After saving a Barred Owl from being attacked by a murder of Crows in the winter of 2023, and bringing it to a local Raptor Center where it was treated for a broken wing and head injury and later released, it has become Laura's mission in life to be able to help animals have a voice. She continues to help them heal emotionally, mentally, spiritually or physically by using the tools she has available to her, alongside working with their human guardians to facilitate in any way they are able to, including seeking the help of veterinary or behavioral professionals when necessary.

So many humans believe that they are superior to all other creatures, but this belief is far from the truth. Animals have always remained able to communicate with other species by using their intuitive senses. It is Laura's goal to help reawaken humans, by sharing insights from their animal companions; to give them a voice that humans in their life can receive.

121

CULTIVATING LUCK: THE POWER OF CURIOSITY AND OPENNESS

by Monica Laurence

PURPOSE: *This exercise will shift your clients into a more expansive, open and curious way of engaging with the world. Social science reveals that luck results from lucky behaviors – such as curiosity, resilience and trusting intuition. When we adopt these behaviors, we observe a quickening of synchronicities. For entrepreneurs, innovators and leaders, this practice can spark new opportunities, new connections and partnerships, and accelerate ventures.*

Is luck random? Or is it possible to influence luck in our lives? It turns out, you can train yourself to be lucky, beginning with a simple shift in behavior.

Welcome to the grind, High Achiever!

By many measures, I have been successful in life. I started working at age 16 and I put myself through top university and graduate programs. I earned my degree in Computer Science and my MBA in Entertainment and Strategy. I worked at Accenture in New York City and Paris, designing the systems to automate stock trades at the Bourse. I joined Lucasfilm at the height of the Star Wars franchise, and my corner office overlooked Skywalker Ranch. And then as the Internet took off, I joined the founding team of a venture-backed Silicon Valley tech startup. Founding and growing companies that shape our world became my new and enduring love.

But how was I doing it all? I was grinding.

I was trained as a high achiever. You may recognize some of these nuggets of common wisdom dished out to high performers — aim high, yet set realistic goals; anticipate and rise above challenges; stay focused and adhere to a strict regimen; expect excellence and set a high-velocity cadence. Lastly, push yourself. Push, push, push.

I call this way of achieving *paddling*. Because when you're on a paddle board, you use your own energy to get from here to there. You set your sights on your target, and then you paddle like crazy. And unsurprisingly, you lose steam and often burn yourself out.

It struck me that there must be a better method for becoming successful.

From Paddling to Surfing

Decades ago I picked up an article. The premise fascinated me. The author wondered if there were differences between lucky and unlucky people.[1] He devised a simple social science experiment and discovered that lucky people *behave differently* from unlucky people. Moreover, when you adopt lucky behaviors, you become luckier. I was captivated and quickly identified that I was behaving like an unlucky person, mostly because I had been trained as a high achiever. I was paddling.

Let me explain.

As the unlucky and lucky people arrived for the experiment, they were handed a newspaper and instructed to count the number of photographs in the paper. They were

1 Dr Richard Wiseman, The Luck Factor - Changing Your Luck, Changing Your Life: The Four Principles, 2003.

assessed for both speed and accuracy. The faster and more accurate the count, the higher the score.

Excellent.

To my surprise, unlucky people tackled the task exactly how I would have tackled the task. Ready, set, go. 5 photographs on page 1, flip to page 2, 3 photographs on page 2, now on to page 3 with 4 photographs, for a tally of 12 and so forth, all the way to the end. Ta-da. Photographs counted and in a few minutes.

Come to find out, that's not how a lucky person does the task. The lucky person starts by counting the photographs on page 1. And then may get distracted by an article. "Oh look, there was a fire downtown! I wonder what happened?" Suddenly the lucky person is reading the article rather than counting the photographs. Doesn't sound so lucky, does it?

But on page 2 was a huge headline: YOU CAN STOP COUNTING - THERE ARE 43 PHOTOGRAPHS. Lucky people routinely saw the headline. And voila, they completed the task in record time, and with 100% accuracy. *Quantifiably*, lucky people had better results. Unlucky people rarely saw the headline. They were too busy being hyper-focused on the task at hand.

When we act with tunnel vision, we miss opportunities in our environment, important opportunities. Opportunities like lucky timing, key connections, or new insights that could benefit us, are most often identified when we adopt a broader perspective.

When I read this article decades ago, a light bulb went off for me. I realized that it may be possible to tap into a different way of being to become successful, namely, to stop paddling and instead start *surfing* with the energy surrounding us.

From Effort to Effortless

The first behavior of lucky people is curiosity and openness.

As children, we are naturally curious. We pepper our parents with questions such as, why is the sky blue? Where does the sun go? What makes a rainbow? Yet by the time we are adults, we accept the world as it is and we stop being curious. We craft to-do lists for ourselves, relishing that hit of dopamine and satisfaction when we tick off the next task, feeling presumably one step closer to our goals.

However, we are not truly in the moment. We are no longer noticing and remain unaware, which then causes us to be unlucky. We are so busy *making things happen* that we miss the openings for serendipity to strike. Strangely enough, we've been trained to operate in this way. To be successful, we are told to focus and work tirelessly.

The science reveals, however, that you can experience delightful serendipity simply by being curious, open and aware. Lucky people are inquisitive and present, even when under stress or time pressure. The newspaper headline was there for everyone, but only the people who were engaged in lucky behaviors were likely to see the headline.

By adopting a behavior of curiosity, you can achieve results in an effortless way.

Like everyone else, I thought luck was random. Surely there was no way to be predictably lucky. However, the social science in that article said otherwise, revealing that it is specific behaviors that make you lucky.

Whaaaaat?

It's true. **Adopt lucky behaviors and you become luckier.** You glide through life with delightful synchronicities. With a smile on your face and exuberance in your step, you have more energy to bring your visions to life.

The Inescapable Equation: Luck as the Key to Success

So now we know that it's possible to be predictably lucky — very cool, and intriguing. How important is this realization? Read on to find out.

In 2022 three mathematicians and physicists won the IG Nobel in Economics for their mathematical proof that luck is essential for success.[2] They discovered that it's not the smartest, most talented or diligent who rise to the top. The people who become exceptionally successful are lucky; and according to the evidence, the optimal combination for stratospheric success is to be moderately talented and magnificently lucky.

What would life be like if you could be *magnificently* lucky? What could you create? What positive impact could you have in our world? Just imagine.

It's time to get lucky.

The Art of Noticing: Everyday Luck and Opportunities Unveiled

Start by being open and training yourself to notice everyday luck.

I'm sure you're already lucky. Maybe you notice. Maybe you don't.

---

2 Alessandro Pluchino, Alessio Emanuele Biondo and Andrea Rapisarda, *Talent Versus Luck: The Role of Randomness in Success and Failure*, 2018.

Everyday luck is often fleeting. We feel charmed in the moment when we experience serendipity. However, if asked to recall examples of our everyday luck from the past week, we're stumped. Your mind may reflect, "I know something cool and unexpected happened, now what was that?"

For me, lucky coincidences happen all the time. Last week I was eating dinner with my sister and her two sons. Her eldest wanted milk for breakfast and negotiation ensued. Finally, my sister gave in and she set off to the store for milk. I offered to walk with her and just as we were exiting the grocery, her neighbor walked by. My sister had been wanting to introduce us. It was a lucky coincidence and all because we went out for milk.

I'm sure you can recall your own lucky moments. Many of you must have experienced thinking of a friend, and then looking down at your phone to see that friend calling you. Or perhaps in the moment of craving an ice cream with childlike desire, you find yourself walking by a shop with your favorite flavor on special.

As I prepared my TEDx talk — *You Need Luck to Succeed* — I reflected on stories of everyday luck. Some people think that everyday luck isn't profound as it does not feel significant to them.

I want you to know a powerful truth. **Noticing and cultivating your everyday luck is your onramp to being bountifully lucky**. And you can start now.

Becoming a Luck Magnet: Your Daily Practice for Serendipity

At this link you'll find a lucky journal - https://quantumsurfing. com/#be-lucky. Download and print the journal for yourself, and then start noticing your own lucky moments. Record the details. Notice how you were feeling, what happened before and what happened after.

As you progress, launch experiments. Play with your ability to be open, curious and in the flow of luck. To become more open and curious, you might try these ideas to start. And as you progress, undoubtedly you'll devise your own methods as well.

1. **Add variety.** To get your brain off autopilot and notice more, mix up your day. For example, go to a new coffee shop, walk to the grocery store or drive a different route to work.

2. **Make it a game.** Try moving through your day or experience as if you're playing a game. For example, if you're going to a gathering, choose a color and talk to everyone wearing that color.

3. **Take action on nudges.** If someone comes to mind, reach out. This week I was at a cafe and overheard two guys speaking about one of my friends. I pinged my friend, and now we have a breakfast date on the calendar. Likewise, I saw an article on a Supreme Court ruling that reminded me of a colleague. I flicked the link to him, and now we have a meetup booked as well.

4. **Notice synchronicities.** (*Hint: This is the big one!*) Jot down serendipities that occur throughout your day. Pay attention to occurrences where you ostensibly did nothing (or did you?), for that uncanny coincidence to materialize. These moments are easy to miss, but once you get the hang of it, you'll realize that lucky moments are happening all the time.

   Some examples:

   a. I was out to dinner with a friend during the

pandemic and we were both missing live music. Later that evening, an unrelated friend in Australia sent me a link to a new band, and the music was awesome. Ask and you shall receive.

b. While out to lunch with a family member, in a town we used to live in, he commented that he'd really love to see friends we knew from baseball games. Just 20 minutes later, we were walking down the street, and there were our friends. What a wonderful reunion.

c. I was strolling with a friend. We had been sending each other texts, but we weren't receiving those texts. So we stopped on the sidewalk to fiddle with phone settings, and we couldn't figure it out. Then my friend looked up and realized that we were standing in front of a phone repair shop. Haha — what are the chances? We popped in and moments later we were able to text each other.

d. I told a mastermind group that I wanted to spend more time with entrepreneurs in Silicon Valley. Seven hours later I got a message on LinkedIn offering me complimentary tickets to an upcoming startup conference.

As you cultivate curiosity and launch experiments, don't forget to jot down your experiences in your journal. This is how you train yourself to notice. Here are some tips for daily journaling:

1. Have fun. Be playful. See what comes.

2. If in doubt, refer to tip #1. 😊

3. Score how lucky your day was. No luck? Give it

a 1. Unbelievably lucky? Give it a 10.

4. Describe the event. What happened?

5. Record your observations. Note the context of your lucky experience. What was your state of mind before your luck flowed in? And your energy? For example, I often find that synchronicities occur rapidly when I desire something in passing, without being attached.

6. To draw attention to your energy and mood, color in your daily mood meter. Ebullient? You're at the top of the scale. Spitting fire? Well, you'll find that face at the bottom.

7. Jot down any experiments you may be inspired to launch next.

Stop paddling. Start surfing.

Luck isn't really all that random. It results from behaviors.

Here I have invited you to be more curious, more open, and more aware of the subtleties in your environment. Luck is infinitely expansive and there are countless more lucky behaviors to experiment with, such as resilience, positive expectations, trusting yourself via intuition, and playfulness.

Many approaches to personal growth begin by trying to convince you — and your analytical mind — that something unexpected is possible. I prefer to start with behaviors. It's easy, even fun, to try new behaviors. And when something is fun, we are eager to explore.

Your beliefs drive your thoughts, which drive your behaviors, which result in your feelings, which reinforce your beliefs. It's a cycle. **You can optimize your cycle by modifying behaviors**.

When those new behaviors produce results, then you and your brain can have a chit-chat about what's *really* going on.

And you can gleefully shift from paddling to surfing.

Monica Laurence

Entrepreneur Strategist, Advisor + Mentor

Location: Virtually, West Coast USA, Europe + Fiji Islands

www.monicalaurence.com, @monicalaurence

www.quantumsurfing.com, @quantumsurfing

www.tavolafiji.com, @tavolafiji

Monica Laurence teams with founders to craft bold strategies for breakthrough success, paired with mindset training for savvy execution, and distinctive style guidance to command authority and build venture value. Monica is a global entrepreneur, TEDx speaker and the

founder of Quantum Surfing — lucky mindset training to transform cutting-edge ideas into reality. She is fascinated by patterns in spirituality, quantum mechanics and neuroscience to understand how our world really works. Monica has been a Silicon Valley tech startup CEO, CMO and Advisor, significantly influencing and shaping 50+ startups. She is an experienced exec in technology and entertainment, and a multi-national leader at Lucasfilm, Disney and Accenture. A natural explorer with a passion for adventure, Monica launched her boutique resort Tavola in the Fiji Islands where she gathers leading-edge thinkers and doers. She brings to this eco-paradise her love of design, fashion and global influences, making Tavola an oasis and international compound of laughter and joy.

Monica holds a BS in Computer Science from Bucknell University and an MBA in Strategy and Entertainment from the Anderson School at UCLA.

TELEPATHY INCREASES YOUR ABILITY TO HELP OTHER SOULS

by Ditte Young

Telepathy is a phenomenon that involves the direct transmission of thoughts, feelings, or information from one person's mind to another's, without the use of any known senses or communication methods.

The term, "telepathy" is derived from two Greek words: "tele", meaning "distant", and "pathos," meaning "feeling" or "perception". The concept suggests direct mental communication that bypasses conventional sensory channels, such as speech or the written word.

You do not have to be born with a special gift to be able to practice telepathy. Telepathy is something we all have access to, particularly when we lower our brain waves and make contact with all other five senses, which include: :

- Sight (vision)
- Sound (hearing)
- Smell (olfaction)
- Taste (gustation)
- Tactile (touch)

By practicing meditation daily, you can easily activate your five senses and become more intuitive and open to activating telepathy. When you start visualizing things in front of your inner eyes, while opening the center of your heart, you begin working with the pineal gland in your brain.

The pineal gland is like a muscle that requires training to become stronger, faster, or stay activated when you use it.

You are likely familiar with the experience of thinking of a person and then receiving a call from that person minutes later. It is a coincidence, to begin with. When you start practicing telepathy, there will not be any coincidences anymore, and you will slowly start to trust your skills.

As a skilled coach or practitioner, you will ask the right questions that guide your client to answer their own question. By asking the right questions, you mirror your clients, allowing them to feel safe and seen. Immediately after you start actively using telepathy, your abilities to sense the client and, therefore, ask the right questions, will heighten.

Telepathy will also advance your skills in empathy. You will begin to not only understand your client but actually sense and feel your client's inner world. It then becomes impossible to project or generate any advice that is outside your client's best interest.

We all want to be understood, seen, and to know that we belong to someone or someplace. In the search for a sense of belonging, we find ourselves constantly attracted to people who share our mindset, or inner values. Unconsciously, our coping strategies are to either adapt to the people we surround ourselves with in order to fit in or to choose like-minded people to surround us.

Can you imagine a world where we can cope with all people, regardless of differing perspectives on the world we all share? Can you imagine a different perspective on how we see things or the world we live in? Using telepathy, we no longer project or have resilience towards a task, other people we meet, or life situations. We can adopt a genuinely observational role in any situation because we truly understand and feel the other soul standing before us.

The minute we mirror and understand another soul, we are helping this person to become more in tune with their heart and emotions. The soul is receptive to this because all souls yearn for a deeper connection with the self and others, as well as to be truly seen in authenticity and with empathy.

Such a framework is how development takes place in any professional situation.

As you work with telepathy, you experience obstacles with others, as obstacles reflecting in your own soul, regardless of whether you embrace it or try to unconsciously suppress it.

This means you can apply any telepathic advice you offer to your client, equally in your own life. You begin to realize that any situations that beckon your help, are in fact, a gift to yourself. Rather than becoming burnt out from helping others, you are energized by the exchange.

We all know that to help other people, we need to help ourselves first. What if we focused on helping ourselves while helping others? When you focus on the dynamic as reciprocal, a different flow will emerge in your sessions, and every client will help raise your vibration instead of depleting your energy.

If you are interested in further exploring the idea of telepathy or want to develop your intuitive and empathic abilities, here are some suggestions:

Meditation: Regular meditation can help you develop a clearer mind and greater sensitivity to your thoughts and emotions, as well as improve your ability to pick up on the thoughts and feelings of others.

Mindfulness: Being present and fully engaged in your interactions can help you become more attuned to non-verbal cues, body language, and emotions.

Empathy: Practice putting yourself in another's shoes and try to understand their feelings and thoughts. This practice can enhance your ability to connect with others on a deeper level.

Intuition: Trust your gut feelings and pay attention to your instincts. Sometimes, we can pick on subtle signals we were consciously unaware of.

Practice with a partner: Find a willing partner interested in telepathy, or in developing intuitive abilities. You can try simple exercises, like sending and receiving mental images or thoughts to one another. Their feedback will help you to understand how you transmit and download telepathy.

Keep a journal: Write down your experiences, thoughts, and any perceived connections with others. This can help you track your progress and notice patterns. For example, you may see symbols or colors, you may hear information, or you may have an intuitive 'knowing'.

Stay open-minded: Being open to the idea that subtle, non-verbal communication can enhance your interpersonal skills and overall understanding of human and/or animal interaction.

Remember that being a good spiritual coach involves ongoing personal and professional growth. It is a commitment to the well-being and development of the individuals you coach, and it requires both knowledge and a genuine desire to help others on their spiritual paths.

I wish you a happy journey in the world of telepathy to widen your horizons and make your talents even greater.

Ditte Young

Known as Denmark's most recognized animal communicator

Worked as a spiritual coach, therapist, and clairvoyant for over 25 years

TedX speaker

Location: Denmark

https://ditteyoung.net/

I was born a sensitive soul with the privilege of being able to sense the spiritual work as a telepath, animal communicator, clairvoyant, and coach. It is a rare gift I was born with because I practice telepathy faster and in much more detail than many other practitioners do. An accuracy of 99 % on each session creates an even greater audience and interest in these abilities, which I am happy to pass on to other interested people. I have taught my telepathic methods to more than 500 people worldwide. Muusmann Publishing has published my knowledge and theory in 3 books about animal behavioral issues, and one book for parents with children who suffer from depression and anxiety, and are neurodivergent or neurotypical. I travel worldwide to broaden people's perspectives and knowledge that behavioral issues are easy to fix and do not exist, as long as we truly understand the needs and structure of the individual condition, being two or four-legged. I have succeeded in spreading my theory and name all over Europe, and I see significant interest from other countries such as the USA, Greece, Spain, England, India, etc. My life's mission is to make telepathy the new big thing because it is all about trusting your intuition. You will become whole as a soul when you can do that.

TIME BENDING: A FRAMEWORK AND EXERCISES FOR UNDERSTANDING AND MANIPULATING TIME

by Derek Loudermilk

"A wizard is never late, nor is he early. He arrives precisely when he means to"

\- Gandalf the Grey, Lord of the Rings

In this chapter, you will learn to change your relationship with time, in order to be more efficient. This will allow you to be more productive, be in the right place at the right time, start things at the right time, finish things on time, have time to do all the things you love, and fit more life into the time you have.

This is for anyone who has ever felt overly busy, lacking enough hours in the day to get everything done, or generally desiring more time.

Benefits: Living life to the fullest, enhanced enjoyment of the journey through time, and ever-increasing personal productivity.

Introduction

For many years, I traveled the world as a professional adventurer and digital nomad. I traveled to dozens of countries, visited sacred sites, immersed in local tribes, sat with shamans, and began to have a series of mystical experiences.

This was the catalyst for my "metaphysical quest" to learn and experience 100 different metaphysical, esoteric, and healing techniques from different traditions around the world. I recently completed my 100th technique as of July 2023 (you can review the full list of experiences on my website if you are curious). A particularly intriguing technique I learned is the ability to play with time. Time bending, time travel, and time manipulation are all not only possible but also quite fun!

Virtually everyone I know wishes they had more time. As a quantum business coach, I have the opportunity to test which techniques from my quest are most relevant to the world of 3D entrepreneurship. In this context, working with time is quite diversely useful. To illustrate, I'll share my first couple of successful time-bending experiments with you:

The first time I was able to bend time, I needed to get a workout at the gym and be home in time for dinner. I was able to fit my travel to and from the gym and an extra long 2.5-hour workout in those 75 minutes, and I arrived home precisely on time.

In my second experience of time bending, I needed to pick up my kids at 3:30 pm. I set up an all-day cycling expedition to another state. In the time after lunch, we completed our transit time and several hours of riding. Ultimately, we arrived at the exact moment my kids were walking out of school (which turned out to be five minutes early), without ever consulting a clock (this is actually a key component to freeing yourself from the normal constraints of the flow of time. More on this in a moment).

I will start by giving you a framework for understanding how time functions for humans, then some practice exercises, so you can begin to bend time for yourself.

In my Quantum Business Mastermind, called the League of Superconductors, we operate from a principle of *working from infinite possibility*. To achieve infinite possibility, one must be free from attempts to control the trajectory of the future or shape the present based on stories of the past. This allows the present to become the fullest expression of what is possible, and thus we begin to manipulate time through our experience of the present moment. For time bending to work best, let go of your stories about how time must be experienced.

How to think about Time:

I'll start with the most important, overarching concepts that you need to know about time, and then explore a few components here to help you prepare for the exercises. As a human, you have two different and simultaneous experiences of time. One is "linear time", wherein moments seem to occur one after the other in a forward movement. The other is "Infinite Soul Time", which is the experience your soul is having. We can think of these as body time and spirit time. The body and soul come together to form a dual timeline by mutual agenda. Think of this as two entangled spirals of expansion, that represent the growth of the spiritual and physical parts of you.

The Greeks called these terms *Chronos* and *Kairos*; quantitative time vs. qualitative time. *Chronos* is a mechanical, second-by-second experience of time, whereas *Kairos* is an experience of time that is full of life. Hint: If you spend more of your chronos doing things that are in alignment with your divine purpose in this lifetime, the 3D measure of productive output will be exponentially higher.

A sunflower is a useful visualization to understand these two perspectives of time. The flower as a whole can represent the "oversoul," which is the point of perspective of the "eternal soul," the perceiver of all incarnations simultaneously. All the different seeds in the face of the sunflower represent the physical incarnations connected with that oversoul - with each one experiencing its own linear time. The perspective of your soul's awareness can "zoom in" to a single lifetime, or "zoom out" to all lifetimes. Einstein was right on target when he realized that time was relative to the point of observation.

So you might ask yourself - is there a benefit to linear time? Yes! When you incarnate into a body, you get to experience a set of experiences only available when you have your five senses and physicality. An incarnation itself creates a gravitational experience or a densification of consciousness that allows the experience of time, and the themes related to that go with that specific lifetime.

Even though we perceive time moving forward as a cause and effect, domino-type experience, research in retrocausality has proven that actions can also change outcomes going backwards in time. My favorite experiment is the retrocausal energy healing experiment, performed 10 years into the past with patients that had hospital-acquired infections. The experimenters split these patients into two groups and gave healing to one group through time. The treatment group had much better outcomes than the control group - they got out of the hospital sooner and lived longer and healthier lives after the treatment. (This is the same protocol used to validate the effectiveness of drug treatments).

Collectively, humans have agreed to measurements of seconds, minutes, and hours. Initially, this would have been to know when to plant and harvest crops, hunt, etc.

144

Time would have been viewed as a circle - such as the cyclical nature of the seasons, the moon phases, the daily cycle, etc. Philosophically, time can also be perceived as a spiral - a Fibonacci spiral moving outwards from the point of origination, but encountering similar themes along the way.

The more focus and attention you give to our collective time structure, the more you will be entangled with its effects. Similarly, in meditation, if you simply observe the structure, without attachment, you can begin to loosen its influence on your experience. This is why you must completely ignore the clock during the times you are practicing time bending.

When people feel like they don't have enough time, there are actually several feeling states they are hoping to experience. One is that life feels effortless in its unfolding and that everything is happening precisely as it means to. In other words, people aspire for a feeling of being in flow with the universe. When you begin to do these time-bending exercises, it will be useful for you to tune in with this feeling of flow, and calibrate your state to one of peaceful happiness.

Your Time Bending Exercises:

1. Begin with a few minutes of Metta meditation (loving-kindness) to calibrate your level of emotion. Send love to members of your family, pets, friends circle, acquaintances, and people you don't know but who may need it, including world leaders. Send gratitude to everything in your world - your house, the air, the water, the directions, the sun, the animals, the ocean, etc. If you have a person or object (talisman) that helps access the feeling of happiness, bring that into

your awareness.

2. Imagine yourself getting more and more dense. On your inhale, feel your physical body getting more dense and heavy, like a stone or a mountain. As you exhale, feel this experience crystalize and get locked in. Use your breath to keep densifying until you are at your most dense. Then, see the face of a clock with the second hand becoming more and more slow moving. Slow down the hands of the clock until time stands still. When time stands still you are in a place of timelessness. Here in timelessness, you will be able to experience more in the same amount of time.

3. Imagine yourself getting lighter and lighter. Feel your physical body filling with light or becoming like steam. Use the in-breath to feel yourself getting lighter, and use the exhale to fix or crystallize this lightness in your physical body. See the second hand of a clock speed up, faster and faster, until it is moving at near-infinite speed. When you hit infinity - you will be in a place of timelessness. Here in infinite time, you will be able to speed up time for things to happen more quickly.

4. Visualize a spiral going upwards like a staircase from your physical body. Walking up the staircase will take you to a future version of yourself in this same incarnation. You can interact with this version of yourself and get guidance about the challenges you are experiencing in the present.

5. Visualize a spiral going downwards. This will take you to an earlier version of yourself in this incarnation.

6. Arrive precisely on time or complete your task precisely on time. This experiment allows you to fit more activity into a specific time. Focus your attention on finishing exactly on time, or arriving at precisely the right moment. You must completely remove any concern or awareness of the clock itself. You will have to put your phone and watch away so that you are not tempted to look at them. Harmonize yourself with the *feeling of being perfectly on time* for your appointment.

7. The "Road Trip Time Jump Technique". For long road trips, as we often take in the USA, you may want to arrive sooner than having to drive a full 14 hours across the middle of the country. There is a specific "feeling state" of arrival. If you want to have a shorter journey, you must harmonize with the feeling-state of arriving at your destination. You may experience a "miraculous" loss of minutes, or even hours, and find yourself driving into town at your destination without being aware of having traveled the roads in between.

You can access the replay of my Live Time Decoder Workshop from my website.

Great for...

• Everyone interested in bending time!

Derek Loudermilk

Quantum Business Coach, Creator of the LEAP method

Host of The Derek Loudermilk Show: Science, Spirituality, and Adventure

Founder of AdventureQuest: transformational adventure retreats

4X Bestselling Author, *Superconductors: Revolutionize Your Career and Make Big*

Things Happen, Activate Your Life, Better Business Book

Location: St. Louis, Missouri/Global

Website: www.derekloudermilk.com

Derek has coached global influencers, leading scientists, cutting-edge entrepreneurs, billionaires, world record athletes, thought leaders, NYT bestselling authors, and high achievers around the world for more than 18 years. His work has been featured in over 100 publications and podcasts globally. Since 2018, Derek has facilitated The League of Superconductors - The world's first quantum business mastermind.

Derek Loudermilk is a former pro cyclist and extreme microbiologist turned professional adventurer, author, and lifestyle entrepreneur. He traveled the world for seven years as a digital nomad, with his family, living in 15 countries during that time. He recently completed a quest to learn 100 different healing, metaphysical, and esoteric practices from around the world.

His podcast, the Derek Loudermilk show, which celebrates its 10th anniversary in 2023, brings people to a high-level understanding of cutting-edge topics in science, spirituality, adventure, and human potential.

PART 4

RELATIONSHIP TO PERSONAL GROWTH AND BUSINESS EMPOWERMENT

THE JUNIOR INFLUENCER'S GUIDE TO GREATNESS

by Logan Griffith

In today's fast-paced world, greatness isn't just about age or experience; it's about perspective, passion, and the will to make a difference. As you dive into this guide, you'll discover the secrets of Logan, a 12-year-old junior influencer, who is already making waves in the world. More than just a guide, Logan serves as a testament to the fact that age is just a number when it comes to achieving greatness.

Great For People Who:

- Are curious about how a young mind views success and personal growth
- Want actionable steps to unlock their potential, regardless of age
- Are ready to challenge their preconceptions and embrace a fresh perspective on personal development

---

Hi there, it's me, Logan Griffith! I'm 12 and I'm not just your average teenager. I am a professional speaker, coach, mastermind leader, course creator, videographer, editor, and best-selling author. At the age of 10, I earned the title of the world's youngest mastermind leader. I proudly led the first Junior Mastermind every week for 90 days, and it was a roaring success. Now, I'm gearing up for the second edition!

You might be wondering, "why should I take advice from a 12-year-old junior influencer?" My unique experiences and achievements, and at such a young age, have given me a perspective that's both fresh and seasoned. The world is a fascinating place, and each one of us is capable of achieving remarkable things. I'm here to provide you with a toolbox of ideas that can help you tap into your potential, and shine your light brightly.

Step 1: Power Up with an Early Rise

Embrace the morning. When the world is quiet, your mind is at its clearest. This is the time when legends are born and dreams take flight.

I've always found that my days are supercharged when I start them with purpose and energy. Whether it's hitting the gym or taking an early morning hill climb, there's something magical about those first rays of sunlight. As I ascend the hill, with each step, I visualize my goals, my successes, and the impact I want to make in the world. More than mere physical exercise, my morning routine is a mental and spiritual one. By the time I reach the top of my climb I'm not only greeted by a breathtaking view, but also a clearer vision of my path forward. I encourage you to find your own early morning ritual, one that aligns with your passions and dreams.

Assignment: For the next month, wake up one hour earlier than usual. Use this extra time to focus on a passion project, personal growth, or simply to enjoy the peace of the early morning.

Step 2: Harness the Power of Positivity

Every challenge is a disguised opportunity, waiting for the right perspective to unveil it. Positivity is the lens that transforms obstacles into stepping stones. I recall a time at a friend's gathering when we were wrestling for fun. I felt confident in my skills, but then there was this one kid who beat me easily. Upon learning he had trained in jiu-jitsu, rather than feeling discouraged, I saw it as an open door. Motivated by example, I began practicing jiu-jitsu myself, while embracing the chance to enhance my skills and grow. The importance here lies not in the setbacks themselves, but rather how you respond to them. Always look for the lesson, or silver lining, and allow it to guide you forward.

Assignment: For the next two weeks, every time you encounter a setback, write it down. At the end of the week, reflect on each and write down a positive outcome or lesson you derived from it. Continue to look for greater and greater opportunities to greet with positivity. .

Step 3: Aim High with Goal-Setting

Set your sights high and do not be afraid to dream big. When you aim for ambitious goals, the journey itself becomes a path of growth. Dreams, when nurtured, can evolve into incredible achievements. Always remember, if you shoot for the stars, you might just make it past the moon.

One of my coolest experiences was during the 'Bay to Breakers' race. My dad and I had this wild idea: What if we could high-five 10,000 people in just one day? So, with a team of 10, we cheered on the racers, celebrating their achievements with high-fives. The response was amazing! Newspapers, Television crews, and news networks broadcasted me to millions. The following day at school, I felt like a mini-celebrity, and found myself signing autographs for my classmates.

The message behind our idea was simple: pay it forward and spread kindness. When you shine your light, the world notices. I have learned that the deepest potential lies not in seeking approval from everyone, but rather in connecting with the right people. So, dream big, share your message, and let your light guide others to you. The world is waiting!

Assignment: Envision a dream so big it inspires you. Break it down into monthly milestones for the next year. Commit to achieving the first milestone within the next 30 days.

Step 4: Action, Effort and Rock-Solid Work Ethic

Dreams create the plan, but it's action that brings them to life. Every big win begins with the choice to step up, put a stick in the sand, and make it happen.

I was inspired by my dad, who was running masterminds for adults. Seeing him lead and teach made me wonder, "Why not create something similar for kids like me?" This is how the idea of running a Junior Mastermind took root. The thought of teaching and leading up to 25 kids every week for 90 days, was both thrilling and challenging. I was determined. I set a start date, gathered my resources, and launched the mastermind. Every week, for an hour, we came together, sharing insights and growing as a group. My mastermind was more than just teaching; it exemplified commitment, consistency, and passion to make a positive impact. When you are inspired by a vision and back it up with unwavering effort, there is no dream too ambitious to achieve.

Assignment: Think of a goal you have been hesitant to start. Now, list down three reasons or habits that have been stopping you from pursuing this goal. Next, identify a positive action or habit to counteract each habit. For the next 60 days, focus on these positive actions, making them a part of your daily routine. As you progress, journal your experiences and note the changes you observe in your mindset and achievements.

Step 5: Strengthen Your Mindset

Pushing past your comfort zone is where real growth begins. Facing challenges head-on showcases the resilience we all carry within.

I'll never forget my first seminar as a speaker. The nerves were so overwhelming that I threw up just moments before I was supposed to go on stage. But I didn't let that stop me. Just five minutes later, I found myself in front of 30 eager faces, sharing my knowledge and passion. It was a clear reminder that sometimes, our biggest obstacles are the ones we create in our minds. Once we overcome these self-imposed obstacles, we are capable of achieving so much more than we ever imagined.

Assignment: Identify one fear that has been holding you back and confront it head-on this month. Whether it's public speaking, rock climbing, or starting a blog, face your fear with courage.

Step 6: Level Up Your People Skills

In today's digital world, real and genuine connections stand out like gold. It's so important to reach out directly to the people you look up to. Once in my Junior Mastermind group, I assigned participants the task of reaching out to the people they admire. Leading by example, I made a list of my top 5 heroes and contacted each of them. Guess what? One of them was the world-famous Dean Graziosi, and he actually responded back to me! This goes to show that you never know what can happen until you try.

Assignment: Identify five individuals whom you deeply admire. Create a personalized strategy to reach out to each of them. Over the next month, initiate genuine conversations with at least three of them, and aim to build a meaningful connection.

Step 7: Embrace Entrepreneurship

In the modern world, the ability to generate multiple streams of income is invaluable. Entrepreneurship isn't just about building businesses, it's about spotting opportunities and seizing them.

I have personally experienced the power of entrepreneurship, earning money as a speaker and coach, and while leading my own mastermind. One of the most exciting moments on my path to entrepreneurship was when I made a video that went viral, reaching 13 million people! Due to its impact, I was even offered a contract. These experiences taught me that when you are passionate and proactive, the opportunities are endless.

Assignment: Over the next month, find a way to earn money outside of a traditional job. It doesn't have to be a large amount; even earning $5 can be a testament to your entrepreneurial spirit. Whether it's selling handmade crafts, offering a service, or leveraging a skill you possess, the goal is to take the first step in understanding the potential of diverse income streams.

So there we have it, your personal road map to greatness. Embarking on this journey may seem daunting, but remember, every giant redwood tree starts as a tiny seed. Plant the seeds of greatness within you and nurture them with these steps. In time, you shall grow into the amazing person you were always meant to be.

This isn't just about achieving success - it's about unlocking the greatness that's already within you. We all have a unique light within us that waits to shine brightly. As we wrap up this chapter, I encourage you to take these steps to heart, for they are the beginning of your journey to greatness.

Thank you for sharing this journey with me. I've seen the spark in so many, and I see it in you too. Remember, greatness isn't just about being the best; it's about bringing out the best in those around you. The world doesn't just need your light, it thrives on it. So, let's make a promise to ourselves and to each other: let's shine, let's inspire, and let's make a difference, together!

Congratulations on diving deep into this chapter and taking steps towards unlocking your inner greatness! To continue this journey and gain even more insights, I invite you to visit https://juniorinfluencers.com. On my website, you will find a free PDF download and exclusive access to a special mini-course crafted to amplify your potential.

Thank you for joining me on this adventure. Always remember, the world is ready to witness your brilliance. Shine on!

Logan Griffith

Logan Griffith, a dynamic 12-year-old from Orange County, California, embodies a blend of youthful zeal and mature insight. Holding the title of the world's youngest mastermind leader, Logan has dedicated more than half of his life to studying and imparting personal growth principles. His prime objective is to assist individuals, regardless of age, in confronting their fears and chasing their grandest dreams.

With titles of Speaker, Coach, Author, Mastermind Leader, and Course Creator under his belt, Logan exhibits a unique aptitude for demystifying complex concepts, making them accessible to a broad audience. His prowess in public speaking, leading masterminds, crafting videos, and coaching reveals a maturity that sets him apart.

Logan spearheaded the Junior Impact Mastermind, a

unique platform that saw him lead over 25 members for more than 90 days, facilitating a space for collaborative growth and learning. His inventive 'Heroes and Monsters' concept has resonated widely, aiding individuals in tackling the fears that hinder them from pursuing their aspirations.

Logan's teaching endeavors extend to live videos, some of which have gone viral, amassing views from millions of individuals worldwide. He's also an engaging live speaker, having addressed diverse groups on numerous occasions. His humanitarian side shines through his regular efforts in feeding the homeless, a practice he's upheld almost every Friday for years.

Logan's positive energy reverberated nationally when he high-fived 10,000 people in one day, capturing media attention. Mentorship from esteemed leaders like Joseph McClendon III, Brian Bradley, and Carolyn Rim has enriched his journey, with some even gracing his video sessions.

As Logan preps for the next cycle of his Junior Impact Mastermind, designed for kids aged 10 to 16, he's also at the helm of launching the Junior Influencer Academy. This academy encompasses a Mastermind, an Online Course, and a 1-on-1 coaching program, all aimed at equipping kids with the tools and strategies needed to make a substantial positive dent in the world.

His forthcoming ventures include his book and workshop, "Heroes and Monsters," further expanding his footprint in the personal growth sphere.

Explore Logan's multifaceted world by visiting LoganGriffith. com. Discover more about the Junior Impact Mastermind at jrmastermind.com.

BREAKING FREE FROM SELF LIMITATION: TRANSFORMING NEGATIVE SELF TALK - ARE YOU HOLDING YOU BACK?

by Sarah Petzold

Within each of us lies an extraordinary power, capable of propelling us toward boundless growth and limitless opportunity. Yet, all too often, this power remains dormant, stifled by the shackles of self-limiting beliefs and negative internal dialogue. Are you holding *you* back? This chapter invites you to embark on a transformative journey that will revolutionize the way you communicate, and how you see yourself, unleashing your true potential.

This is an opportunity to extend a compassionate hand to our younger selves and to become the voice we need when we are at our most vulnerable. As you engage with the following exercises, reflections, and insights, remember that you possess power. Only you can rewrite your internal dialogue, shatter the limitations that have held you back, and embrace your true potential through a journey of healing, growth, and self-discovery. These exercises are designed to ignite your inner power so that you become your own best advocate.

Self Limiting Beliefs

Have you ever considered that one of the greatest hindrances to seizing opportunity is none other than your very own self? Your own internal dialogue can become a relentless critic, bombarding you with self-doubt, worthlessness, and a constant stream of negativity. If you spoke to someone the same way your mind speaks to you, how would they respond? The most common answer I receive to that question is, "They would never speak to me again."

Take a moment to imagine the weight of those negative thoughts, echoing in your mind day and night. How have they shaped your perception of yourself and influenced the decisions you make? How often have they held you back from embracing new opportunities and moving forward in life? Now picture a different scenario–imagine being your own biggest cheerleader, instead of your harshest critic.

Recall a time when you hit rock bottom, when you felt the smallest, weakest, and most insecure. Difficult, potentially traumatic experiences can leave deep imprints on our psyche. What internal narrative plagued your mind during that period? Did that internal voice sound something like, "I'm weak, I'm worthless, I don't deserve happiness, I am not good enough"?

Now, look at where you are today. How many of those negative beliefs from the past have clung to you and infiltrated your present reality? Our perception of the difficult events we experience, as well as how we view ourselves within those events, can contribute to limiting beliefs that hold us captive.

The lens through which we view ourselves and our lives is often colored by a defeatist mindset–a lens that distorts our true potential. But what if we could change it? The benefit of this activation exercise is the healing process that begins when we change our lens, disrupt the negative internal loop, and challenge disempowering beliefs. We can initiate this transformative process with the simple act of writing a letter.

Begin the Transformation

To begin, identify one specific limiting belief that you want to challenge such as "I'm weak," "I'm not good enough," or "I'm worthless." Think back to the earliest moment that you remember having this thought, or where it felt the most profound. Address your letter to this specific version of yourself, and be as detailed as is necessary to truly connect with this self that was impacted by the limiting belief. Now ask yourself, what did this version of you need to hear at that moment in time?

Imagine speaking to yourself as if you were addressing a friend. Write freely for at least five minutes, allowing your thoughts and emotions to flow onto the page. Below is an example:

Dear Frightened me,

I want to tell you that it gets better. I know we have been feeling alone and afraid and we have been running from so much. All of this fear has been holding us back and I need you to recognize this. This fear has kept us stuck, feeling small and weak, and it is time for me to tell you that it's time to let go.

Thank you for shouldering our fears for so long. I know you were just trying to protect us from any more hurt, pain, and abandonment, but now we have arrived at a space where we are safe. You are free to let this go. It's time. Through this hard and long journey, we have arrived. I am here for you. I am here to allow us to take steps forward. You

are strong, you are enough, you are courageous, and you are worth it. You can do this.

Connect with the voice that empowers you at the time that you are feeling small or weak. That empowered version is also inside you. We become so focused on the negative self-talk, that we fail to hear the empowering coach within us.

Through this writing process, common barriers are guilt and shame. Limiting beliefs often get rooted in feelings of guilt spurred by thoughts like, "I should've done this or that". Then shame kicks in and the negative self-talk of "because I didn't do that, I am not good enough" becomes the limiting belief. Here are some questions to ask yourself if these types of thoughts are coming up for you.

Consider a younger version of yourself with empathy. Did you know how to handle the situation any better, or were you doing the best you could with what you knew then? Did you have the tools or the skills to handle the situation any better? Most often, the answer is no. We can challenge negative self-talk when we develop compassion and understanding for our younger selves, and this is the foundation of our letter.

Once you have expressed what your younger self needs to hear, we will take it a step further. Find a mirror or an empty chair and visualize that specific version of yourself standing before you. Imagine, how do they feel right now? What are they wearing? What does their body language convey?

Now, read your letter out loud, directing your words toward this version of you. Feel the emotional impact of your words, as if they were truly being heard by your past self.

Take a moment to reflect on the changes within you. How

do you feel now? What has shifted within you? Do you still believe all that negativity you once told yourself, or have you become more compassionate, understanding, and positive?

Moving Beyond Limitations

In my experience guiding numerous clients through this activation exercise, I have witnessed people develop a new connection with themselves and their younger selves, based on compassion, understanding, and positivity. Ultimately this promotes empowerment and challenges the limiting beliefs that were previously holding the client back. Repeat this exercise as needed to challenge multiple limiting beliefs. The sense of freedom and healing that comes not only from writing the letter but from reading it aloud is well worth it. Saying the words aloud gives them power and emotion, helping the person feel seen and heard, resulting in more healing and growth.

Let us walk toward a future defined by self-empowerment, resilience, and self-discovery. If this stirred something inside you, and you are ready to unlock and challenge limiting beliefs, I encourage you to embark on this healing journey.

At the end of it all, embrace this truth. You are enough. It's time to internalize this belief and allow yourself to soar to new heights of self-acceptance and self-belief. By rewriting your self-talk narrative, you have the power to transform your limiting beliefs and in turn, transform your life from within.

Sarah Petzold

Licensed Social Worker and Certified Trauma Professional

Email: sapetzold2007@gmail.com

Linkedin: linkedin.com/in/sarah-petzold-therapy

Sarah is a compassionate and dedicated private practice therapist, specializing in trauma therapy with a unique focus on Eye Movement Desensitization and Reprocessing (EMDR) therapy. With years of experience and extensive training, Sarah is a trusted professional in the field of mental health, making a meaningful impact in the lives of countless individuals.

Drawing upon a deep well of empathy and clinical expertise, Sarah has dedicated their career to helping those who have experienced the profound effects of trauma. Their commitment to healing and resilience shines through in every therapy session.

One of Sarah's distinctive strengths lies in their work with veterans, first responders, and individuals of all ages, dealing with a wide range of mental health diagnoses and addictions. Their extensive training in EMDR therapy, a cutting-edge and highly effective approach to trauma resolution, has provided life-changing breakthroughs for many.

In addition to their private practice, Sarah is deeply involved in Crisis Intervention Training Programs for First Responders in the Lackawanna County area. Their contributions in this realm have helped equip these brave individuals with the emotional tools and resilience needed to navigate the unique challenges they face daily.

With Sarah's guidance, countless clients have embarked on a journey of self-discovery and healing. They bring a warmth and understanding that helps individuals feel safe and supported throughout their therapeutic journey. Their expertise, combined with their compassionate approach, makes them an invaluable resource for anyone seeking to overcome trauma, find resilience, and reclaim their lives.

When you choose Sarah as your therapist, you are choosing a guide who will walk with you on your path to healing, no matter how challenging the journey may seem. Their dedication and expertise in trauma therapy, particularly EMDR, make them a trusted partner in the process of transformation and growth.

Begin your journey and let's connect!

EMPOWER YOUR MASCULINE INNER LEADER: 5 DAILY QUESTIONS MEN CAN ASK TO ALIGN WITH THEIR HIGHER SELF

by Josef Hortnagl

What is it all about?:

An introductory tool for men to learn about emotional intelligence through adopting 5 sacred masculine oaths, in a daily self-reflection practice.

How does it tie into my X-factor?

My X-Factor is the profound clarity and intuition I have for understanding the confusion that exists in a man's inner world, as well as the collective struggles that manifest in the outer world as a result. I created the Sacred Masculine as a way to share this understanding with all men. Its purpose is to show men the inner and outer causes and effects that are making life so difficult for them, as well as what to do about it.

The Sacred Masculine is focused on dissolving the chaotic web of expectations, double standards, and falsehoods about what it means to exist as a man. Sacred Masculine is a new paradigm for masculinity, forged into a toolset men can use to improve their lives, relationships, and connection to their higher calling. The 5 sacred masculine oaths are a fundamental aspect of the coaching methodology.

How does it serve my future clients?

The daily practice offered in this chapter is a low-risk introduction for men to learn about their masculinity, and how they can utilize it in all aspects of their lives.

What is the ultimate outcome?

To heighten awareness of the sacred masculine and its potential, to attract new one-on-one clients, to attract new customers interested in purchasing courses, and to begin the revolution of masculinity for the benefit of all.

Empower your Masculine Inner Leader

The importance of masculine energy in men's lives has become obscured in today's world. Too many men experience a profound loss of confidence and a deep longing for something more meaningful in life. The remarkable news is that masculine energy is never truly lost and can be rekindled by a simple daily practice.

During my exploration and quest to redefine modern masculinity, I have uncovered five paramount principles that embody the most profound virtues masculine energy offers to men. I refer to these principles as the 5 Sacred Masculine Oaths. As men reflect upon these oaths, an inner leader is unleashed, ready to empower their lives. Embracing these 5 sacred masculine oaths holds the potential to revolutionize masculinity, forging a new paradigm that benefits us all.

Together, we can thrive and prosper by re-establishing the true value of masculine energy.

Let us embark on this transformative journey to better understand masculinity, unlock the power within, and embrace the 5 Sacred Masculine Oaths as the cornerstone of a reinvigorated masculine identity.

Understanding Masculine Energy:

At its core, masculine energy is the vital force that ensures the expansion of life and guides us safely into the future. It possesses an innate ability to penetrate, organize, shelter, and protect the precious essence of its counterpart, feminine energy. Masculine energy weaves the threads of structure, patterns, and systems, providing the nurturing framework necessary for growth and sustainability.

Masculine energy fearlessly confronts the chaotic nature of the universe, bestowing upon it order and meaning. Its very essence can be visualized as points, lines, and edges, shaping space and time into repeating and expanding forms. Through this process, it imparts definition to the world, allowing knowledge and understanding to emerge.

Strength, independence, assertiveness, and logic are among the traits commonly associated with masculine energy. This energy is the driving force that compels us to take action, set ambitious goals, and attain tangible results. It fearlessly faces uncertainty and embraces danger and risk with unwavering courage. Achieving a harmonious alignment with our masculine energy empowers us to set goals, take decisive action, and taste the sweetness of success.

When we lose alignment it manifests as excessive aggression, unhealthy competitiveness, or domineering tendencies. We find ourselves grappling with emotions of anger, frustration, or impatience, indicating we have lost touch with our true masculine energy.

The Five Sacred Masculine Oaths Freedom: To have sovereignty over oneself

For every masculine being, the yearning for freedom resonates deep within. Freedom, when embraced through the lens of sacred masculinity, reveals itself in various forms. It can manifest as solitude, allowing us to eliminate distractions and find clarity and simplicity. It can be found in discipline, organizing, and creating systems for our lives. Surprisingly, freedom can also emerge through commitment, fostering focus, and an unwavering devotion to who and what is dear to us.

The oath to freedom continuously urges the masculine to choose truth. By doing so, we ensure that our expression of reality remains unrestricted and free from the confines of limitations, both within our minds and in the world around us. Ultimately, the most potent embodiment of masculine freedom lies in the power of choice. To fulfill our role as penetrating and transformative energies, we must be completely liberated, and fearlessly taking action.

Embrace the essence of masculine freedom, for it is through this liberation that we unleash our true potential. Freedom and the truth of our choices become a source of empowerment where the masculine spirit soars to new heights.

Service: To provide that which is needed

Masculine essence is synonymous with acts of service, making him a revered and sacred being. The impact of his deeds upon the world is a profound reflection of his purpose. True masculine energy is driven by an instinctive calling to undertake meaningful actions that contribute to the betterment of our world. It is his sacred duty to service that ensures life thrives and prospers.

The masculine spirit is invigorated by witnessing inequities and struggles within the world. It is through the power of the mind that problems are solved, and this is where the masculine finds its purpose in the world. The call to protect what holds deep significance for us resides within the souls of all masculine beings. When we embrace our duty to service, we protect and nurture what is dear to us, allowing our actions to resonate with profound meaning and impact.

Comradery: To be an important part of the whole

Accountability and trust lie at the core of the masculine being, forging profound connections among brethren. It is through this communion that the masculine finds its deepest bonds. Comradery becomes the embodiment of these virtues, where a profound connection grounded in unwavering truth flourishes. Embracing this sacred strength is crucial for the masculine journey.

The concept of the masculine word is rooted in the oath to comradery. It cannot be fabricated or deceived, as it is built upon the purest form of truth known to the masculine spirit. It represents the subtle agreement woven amidst the inherent danger that masculine energy possesses. It is an unspoken commitment to connect and collaborate, fortifying the power to remain steadfast in upholding the other sacred oaths. By embracing the virtues of accountability and trust found within comradery, we unlock the potential for profound growth, collaboration, and unwavering commitment to our shared journey.

Lethality: To master that which needs to be vanquished

The essence of masculinity finds potent expression in its physical nature, particularly in its capacity and inherent need to be lethal. From the moment of first awareness, the masculine has engaged with the world through physical interaction. Mastery over the chaotic forces of nature enables him to accomplish and uphold the other Sacred Masculine Oaths. Without physical capability, one's freedom of movement becomes limited, hindering their ability to act. Without the potential for physical danger, the protection of oneself and others in their domain is compromised. Mastery over skills and tasks empowers the masculine to provide and enrich not only his own life but also the lives of those around him. Masculinity serves as the container, protector, and problem solver. The inability to embody these qualities deeply distresses the masculine soul.

However, while the capability to be physically dangerous is essential, it is crucial to recognize the responsibility of restraint. The masculine must choose between forcefulness and true power, two seemingly similar yet profoundly distinct expressions of lethal potential. Using physical force to dominate others distorts the very essence of the Sacred Masculine Oaths. Force is unsustainable and constantly demanding renewal. To be a tyrant is to become a prisoner, enslaved by an insatiable thirst for more force.

True power lies in upholding the honor and privilege of physical strength and utilizing that strength to uphold the sacred masculine oaths. By exemplifying prowess and exercising restraint, the masculine influences and inspires others to follow suit. The radiance of power emanates from the restrained manifestation of physical, mental, and spiritual lethality, leaving an indelible mark on the hearts and minds of all who encounter it.

Challenges: To be pushed beyond what is known

For the sacred masculine, purpose resides not only in a distant future but also within the challenges of the present moment. The future serves as an anchor for our aspirations and desires yet to be fulfilled. However, it is through a deep-rooted acknowledgement and appreciation for the present, that the masculine finds the strength to propel forward and meet their future self.

To conquer the looming specter of the unknown, the masculine must courageously confront it with open vulnerability and sacrifice. It is within the struggle to surpass familiar boundaries that the energetic power of the masculine springs forth. This power revitalizes both the individual and their surroundings, infusing them with novelty, freshness, and meaningful order. Without a struggle to face, the masculine's energy dwindles, leading to profound distress.

In such circumstances, a masculine being may inadvertently seek out meaningless conflicts or engage in self-sabotage, merely to have something to contend against. It is essential, therefore, that he remains free to perpetually pursue an elevated version of himself. This pursuit is not rooted in vanity but rather enables him to tap into the deep wellspring of life's nourishing energy within himself. As the masculine progresses through the various phases of his lifespan, the nature of these challenges may shift, but the constant pursuit of them remains.

Daily Practice to Reflect on Your Alignment with the 5 Sacred Masculine Oaths

The 5 sacred masculine oaths possess incredible power and practicality. They serve as guideposts, enabling us to embark on a journey of self-reflection and contemplation.

Often, when we examine specific areas of our lives, we find ourselves uncertain about our achievements and failures. This is where the 5 sacred masculine oaths offer us a way of being that brings forth our highest masculine selves. They become a compass, directing us toward the changes we may need in our lives.

To initiate this transformative process, I have provided 5 prompts designed to ignite honest and empathetic self-reflection. By posing these questions to ourselves and truly listening within, the concealed truth will emerge, resonating with the voice of our inner masculine leader.

Embrace the opportunity to explore these sacred oaths, as we embark on a path of self-discovery. Through their guidance, we uncover the keys to a purposeful and fulfilling life, enriched by profound masculine transformation.

- Where in my life do I feel trapped or restricted? What courageous action or vulnerable conversation could I have, that would change these feelings to unhindered freedom?

- Where in my life can I do more for others? What courageous action or vulnerable conversation could I have, to make an impact on those most important to me?

- Where in my life do I feel alone and isolated? What courageous action or vulnerable conversation could I have with a friend, mentor, or community to feel connection and belonging?

- Where in my life do I feel weak or limited? What courageous action or vulnerable conversation could I have that would allow me to become stronger or more capable?

- Where in my life am I avoiding growth? What

courageous action or vulnerable conversation could I have to push beyond a limit, either in my mind, body, or spirit?

Reflect on a daily basis as part of a morning or evening ritual. Keep a journal of your emotions and feelings when reflecting on these questions. Record what your intentions are towards each question to help guide your thoughts and actions. Let this practice become a consistent part of your daily routine and enjoy the powerful changes that occur as you rediscover the power of your sacred masculine.

Josef Hortnagl

Services Offered: Dating, Relationship, and Personal Development Coach for men.

Location: Puerto Vallarta, Mexico

Website: www.thesacredmasculine.com

Facebook, Instagram, TikTok: @Josef_Hortnagl

Josef Hortnagl is a Dating, Relationship, and Personal Development Coach specializing in helping men reconnect with the power of their Masculinity. Josef has been dedicated to spreading knowledge on the energetics of masculine-feminine polarity and how it can improve people's lives, for over half a decade. He has developed "The Sacred Masculine" as a coaching program to help men find greater peace and harmony in their lives. His Goal is to introduce men to a new revolutionary paradigm of masculinity focused on empowerment, inner harmony, and outward achievement for a brighter future.

During his time teaching, coaching, and writing on the topic of men's mental health, he has become well-versed in the psychological methodology of internal family systems and its methods for healing past traumas. He integrates this in work along with other personal development methods, such as emotional intelligence, the law of attraction, the enneagram, gene keys, human design, Power vs Force, and most importantly, masculine-feminine polarity. These powerful tools have helped Josef become a rising leader in the pursuit of helping men and veterans improve their health, relationships, and livelihood.

Josef is also an avid physical fitness and bodybuilding enthusiast and enjoys mentoring and coaching men to reach new levels of health and vitality. After finishing a 15-year career as an engineer, Josef has become a full-time coach with his wife Jordin. The two of them travel the world as digital nomads, currently loving life in Puerto Vallarta, Mexico. They work to support each other and combine their coaching expertise to provide relevant and vulnerable examples, tips, and advice for those who need it.

ACTIVATING YOUR POWER OF CHOICE: MASTERING YOUR MONEY STORY

by Jillian Schleger

Why do so many Entrepreneurs struggle with the feast or famine syndrome?

With the amount of coaches, consultants and healers I've worked with over the years, money is the topic that comes up regularly. Specifically, my clients want to know how they can create more choice and mastery with their money and income.

Is this something that you'd like to feel in control of as well?

This is great for:

- Those feeling disempowered in their relationship to money
- Those looking for an easy and powerful way to change their subconscious beliefs about money
- Anyone who is ready to change negative emotions around money, in order to create a positive financial reality

---

The first thing I ask my clients is how their money story makes them feel. This usually ties back to an early memory of money which created a sense of not having a choice with money.

What is your first memory of money?

I remember hearing my neighbor tell her young daughter that money was dirty after her daughter showed her a nickel that she had picked up from the driveway.

I thought oh boy, what a challenging start to her money story! My money story didn't start out great either. When I was 12, my first job was at a local store. I was too young to even have a bank account, so all of my paychecks had to be signed over to my mother. That was the start of my 'money doesn't belong to me' money story.

Now that I am a solopreneur, I had to look more closely at my money story so that I could change it to work for me. Today, I help other business owners do the same thing, so that they can create their life, business and income on their own terms.

The main challenge I commonly see is a money story that leads my clients to the conclusion that they don't have mastery over money.

In this chapter, I'll give you the best tools and most powerful steps I know of that will empower you to master your money story, in order to feel in control of creating the money you want.

I'm sure you have your fair share of tools, processes and techniques that you've used over the years to break old cycles and patterns and create the life that you want.

But have they truly worked?

You see people go to the same personal development training year after year, and yet they are in the same place that they were the year before, with nothing having changed and their desires remaining unmaterialized. I didn't want that for myself and I don't want that for you.

Wouldn't it be nice to have a tool that pulls back the curtain and allows us to look at the mechanics of what is going on behind the scenes?

If we see that specific block around manifesting what we honestly desire as a needle to hunt down in a big, bad, pile of hay, wouldn't it be fantastic to have a tool that would grant us steps to ignite all of that hay in a wild and wonderful bonfire?

This might allow us to identify what that specific block was so that we could dissolve it in its entirety. We may consciously know how to manifest, and yet when we step up to the plate to manifest the things we really want, those tools fall short. Instead of creating that spark that lights up our bonfire, we might merely see a wee puff of smoke.

Something is getting in the way, that is deep within our subconscious mind. There must be a program that's working behind the scenes, that is keeping us stuck at a certain level.

There is a tool you can use, and this tool doesn't just let you find out what those unconscious, hidden programs are, but it also allows you to change them in such a way that is lasting, easy, effective, and nothing like you've experienced before.

One client of mine, I'll call her Anne (with an E of course, since I live near PEI and have to pay homage to Anne of Green Gables), came to me wanting to quit her day job and start her business. When I asked her what kind of income would allow her to comfortably leave her DJ (Day Job) she had to pause the session for several minutes. She became so physically ill at the mere mention of money that we had to shift gears and eliminate that money trauma before we continued with her business strategy. After one session, Anne went from feeling nauseous at the thought of being in charge of her money story to manifesting the exact number of clients needed to leave her job within days of our session.

How did we know exactly what to look for during that one session?

I connected Anne with her Power of Choice through something called the Kinetic Divination Board (KDB).

We are now going to do some muscle testing so that you can check in with your unique Power of Choice around your money story. To do this, we will set up your Kinetic Divination Board (KDB). Imagine there is a whiteboard out in front of you with 0% on the left and 100% on the right.

Begin populating this whiteboard with things you know to be correct, like your correct name and things you enjoy doing, creating or eating. Then begin to populate the whiteboard with things that you wouldn't ever do, eat or drink. Just play with this, and allow yourself to become aware of any inkling you may have of how the whiteboard reacts to your thoughts.

If you aren't perceiving much, try thinking of something or someone you are grateful for, hold onto that feeling of gratitude for at least 30 seconds, and then try again.

Be in the state of mind that this works for you and can add a dimension of empowerment to your life that you may have not had before. Now, start to think about some areas of your life that you feel you do have mastery over.

Think of things you do that you feel confident and empowered doing.

This could be that you make a mean upside-down

pineapple carrot cake (I know that's totally specific, but that's my go-to favorite cake).

Maybe it's your ability to hold your poker face longer than any of your friends while playing your favorite card game, or the fact that you can draw the best stick figure of all time. This can be anything that is complementary to your unique abilities. Have some fun and compile a short list. I don't want to hear 'But Jillian, I don't have mastery over any area of my life!'

There's always something that you excel at.

If you're truly unsure, call up your favorite friend and ask what they think you're really good at, and if it's that you bake a mean upside-down pineapple carrot cake too, we will definitely have to have a bake-off!

Now that you have a list of what you have mastery over, you're going to check in with the KDB.

Look at the first item on your list and say:

"I have true mastery over _____" and see what percentage comes up.

Then continue on with each item on your list.

Now try the statement: "I have true mastery over creating money" and see what comes up.

Write down the first percentage that comes to mind.

Even if you feel that you have a good relationship with money this percentage may be lower than expected. If it is, I applaud you.

This shows that you are available to look at the true, behind-the-scenes story of your relationship with money.

Consciously, we may see life and our relationships with certain things, people and situations in a certain way.

But subconsciously, those relationships may actually be run by a program that we aligned with, agreed to, and bought many moons ago. These stories sit in our bodies. We can connect with our bodies to change these stories by using our awareness and this KD Whiteboard.

For this next part, we will be changing the programming that has been keeping you stuck at a lackluster money story. Please take responsibility for your own well-being, check with your KD * Whiteboard that this is safe for you to do, and increase your water intake anytime you do this process.

Going forward means you agree to the above.

Cool. Let's change some stuff!

If you were right in front of me, I could intuitively tune-in to feel where your money story is sitting in your body. However, you can do this without the help of an Intuitive Healer, just be open to the awareness of how powerful you are. Take a deep breath, return to your state of gratitude and imagine that whiteboard again. Check in with "I have true mastery over creating money" and become aware of the percentage you get.

Write down the percentage you get.

Now imagine that you can grab that percentage and bring it up toward 100%.

Pay attention to what your body does.

Write down the percentage you get after shifting it up.

If you're super sensitive, spend some time tuning into

what images, feelings and memories that come up after shifting that percentage. You can journal on these things but I suggest not spending too much time on them.

Incorporate the rule:

My intentions and attention are the currency my future requires to thrive.

Test more statements about your relationship with money and begin to change your feeling of ease with money. Eventually, you will create a money story that will allow you to feel in control and have mastery with money.

You can go to the following link to receive an in-depth video of this process as well as some other key money stories to shift out of and positive abundance activations to align and agree with!

https://bit.ly/ActivateBonuses

Key tips for the Coach, Consultant and Healer;

- The KDB will be different for everyone, let your client take his or her time to develop this visual for themselves.

- If your client is having difficulty seeing percentages, it could mean that they're testing something that has a lot of emotional attachment. A centering process can be beneficial in helping them release emotional attachment. I have much success with helping clients release emotional attachment when I use the Alpha Level Breath (Silva Method), and walk my clients through an energetic expansion process. I'll put links to these processes on my Activate Your Power of Choice Bonuses page.

- Alternatively, if your client is not able to perceive a whiteboard or percentages on the KDB, try leading them into a state of gratitude by asking them to think of someplace, some time, or someone whom they are grateful for. The KDB is a tool that allows us to muscle test ourselves. In order for us to muscle test ourselves accurately, our vibration must be at a resonance of courage (200 MZ) or above, as Dr David Hawkins talks about in his book Power vs Force.

Have fun with the KDB! I hope that it creates amazing blessings and shifts for you and your clients!

Jillian Schleger

Intuitive Business Coach; Creator of the Kinetic Divination Healing Methodology (KD)

Founder of the Dynamic Intention Mastermind Program

Author of *Kinetic Divination*, *Dynamic Intention*, the *Dynamic Intention Journal*, *Emergence*, *Sheepish*, and the (soon to be) *Dancing with Shadows* Series with Hay House.

Location: Nova Scotia, Canada/Global

Website: JillianSchleger.com

Jillian has coached heart-led entrepreneurs, creatives, and 5 figure business leaders for over 7 years. This work has been the natural progression and expansion of the healing work she has done for over 30 years. It's the process of teaching tools which effectively allow highly sensitive business owners to receive abundance after becoming their most authentic selves, that lights Jillian up the most.

The tools within KD encourage the confidence and certainty required for Jillian's clients to skyrocket their business, impact and income. While coaching business owners and healers, it was evident to Jillian that an unsettling percentage of the clients she worked with, had debilitating stories around money that held them back from creating the life and business they desired. This propelled Jillian to create a business blueprint that supported more coaches and healers so that they could create an advantageous reality with money.

As a former gymnast and gymnastics coach, Jillian's coaching experience ignited a love of teaching that led her to South Korea. While in Asia, Jillian explored many countries where her affinity for mindfulness and manifestation grew. She is a singer/songwriter, photographer and artist, and much of her free time is spent creating music and art when she is not writing, coaching, or speaking.

THE IMPACT ACCELERATOR

by Ian C. Griffith

Unlock the untapped power within you to amplify your impact and create a legacy of positive change. This transformative chapter serves as your comprehensive guide, offering practical strategies and integrating the groundbreaking capabilities of Artificial Intelligence (AI) to supercharge your journey.

You Will Benefit If You:

- Aspire to Forge Authentic Connections: Learn how to connect authentically with figures you admire, creating partnerships that amplify your message

- Seek to Optimize Efficiency and Impact: Utilize the Pareto Principle and the Eisenhower Matrix to focus your efforts where they matter most, maximizing both efficiency and impact

- Are Ready to Unleash Their Inner Hero: Embrace your unique potential and visualize the transformative change you can bring to your audience and the world at large

- Wish to Harness the Power of AI: Discover how Artificial Intelligence can be a game-changer in accelerating your impact and achieving your goals

---

1. The Foundation: Embrace Your Inner Hero

You are the hero the world is waiting for. This isn't just a motivational statement; it's a call to action:

- **Believe in Your Potential**: Recognize that you possess unique experiences, insights, and value. Your worth is immeasurable

- **Visualize Greater Impact**: Imagine the profound change you could bring by amplifying your influence a thousandfold. Envision yourself making monumental strides and positively impacting countless lives on a scale you never thought possible

- **Take Initiative**: Don't wait for opportunities; create them. Whether it's pioneering a project, reaching out to someone you admire, or sharing your insights, be proactive

- **Inspire Through Action**: Understand that there are countless individuals worldwide who could benefit from your knowledge, passion, and drive. By rising and shining your light, you can make a tangible difference in their lives

- **The World Needs You**: Imagine a world where your actions, no matter how small, create ripples of positive change. By embracing your greatness and shining your light, you become a beacon of hope and inspiration for countless individuals

Assignment: Identify a challenge or issue in your community or industry that you're passionate about. Develop a comprehensive project or initiative to address this challenge. Visualize the massive positive impact your initiative could have and outline the steps, resources, and collaborations needed. Commit to launching this initiative within the next six months, aiming for a transformative impact.

2. The Strategy: Connecting with Key Influencers and Admired Figures

The path to amplifying your influence often begins by recognizing and connecting with those who've already made significant strides in your field. These are not just the influential figures but also those you deeply admire for their work, ethics, and contributions.

- **Identify the Influencers and Admired Figures**: Start by listing influential people in your field, but also include those whose work you genuinely admire. This could encompass industry leaders, trailblazing bloggers, insightful podcasters, or impactful social media personalities

- **Research and Understand Them**: Dive deep into their work, ethos, and passions. This understanding will not only help you connect on a genuine level but also identify areas of potential collaboration or mutual growth

- **Connect Authentically**: A genuine connection goes beyond business pitches. It could be a shared vision, a collaborative idea, or simply an expression of admiration for their work. Authenticity is key

- **Build and Nurture Relationships**: True influence is built on relationships that are mutually beneficial and nurtured over time. Such relationships can lead to collaborations, endorsements, or partnerships, amplifying your influence manifold

Assignment: Identify fifteen key figures in your field - ten influencers and five individuals whose work you deeply admire. Research their contributions and craft a personalized outreach strategy for each. Over the next month, initiate a genuine conversation with at least five of them, aiming to build a meaningful connection.

3. The Execution: Mastering Time and Productivity with The Pareto Principle Funnel

The Pareto Principle, or the 80/20 rule, posits that 80% of the results come from 20% of the efforts. When you apply this principle repeatedly, it forms a funnel, allowing you to narrow down your focus to the most impactful activities and reach the top echelons of efficiency.

- **First Level**: 20% of 168 hours a week is 33.60 hours. This is where 80% of your results come from

- **Second Level**: 20% of those 33.60 hours is 6.72 hours. This is the time frame where you achieve 64% of your results

- **Third Level**: 20% of 6.72 hours is 1.34 hours. Here, you're looking at 51.2% of your results

- **Fourth Level**: 20% of 1.34 hours is roughly 0.27 hours or 16.13 minutes. This tiny fraction of your week, when focused on the most impactful activities, can yield a staggering 41% of your results

- **Fifth Level**: 20% of 16.13 minutes is approximately 3.23 minutes. In this minuscule window, when dedicated to the absolute pinnacle of impactful tasks, you can achieve 32.8% of your results

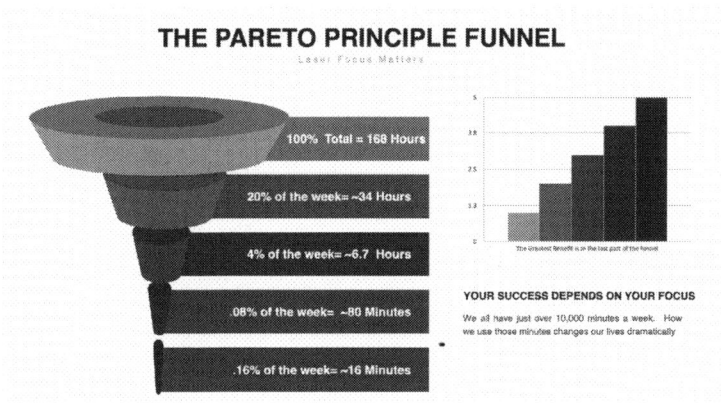

THE PARETO PRINCIPLE FUNNEL

Laser Focus Matters

100% Total = 168 Hours

20% of the week= ~34 Hours

4% of the week= ~6.7 Hours

.08% of the week= ~80 Minutes

.16% of the week= ~16 Minutes

YOUR SUCCESS DEPENDS ON YOUR FOCUS

We all have just over 10,000 minutes a week. How we use those minutes changes our lives dramatically

Assignment: Analyze your past month. Identify the tasks that took up the majority of your time. Apply the Pareto Principle Funnel to determine which activities yielded the most results. Create a detailed action plan for the next three months, focusing on enhancing those top-performing activities and eliminating or delegating the least impactful ones.

4. The Execution: Mastering Time and Productivity with the Eisenhower Matrix:

In the quest to amplify influence and make a lasting impact, productivity plays a pivotal role. The Eisenhower Matrix, a time-tested tool, offers a structured approach to task prioritization, ensuring that you channel your efforts where they matter the most.

Understanding the Eisenhower Matrix:

The Eisenhower Matrix, inspired by Dwight D. Eisenhower's insights on urgency and importance, is a visual tool that categorizes tasks into four quadrants. This categorization helps in determining which tasks to tackle immediately, which ones to schedule for later, which ones to delegate, and which ones to discard.

Benefits of the Eisenhower Matrix:

- **Clarity in Prioritization:** The matrix offers a clear visual representation of where your tasks stand in terms of urgency and importance. This clarity can be instrumental in decision-making and task allocation

- **Enhanced Time Management:** By focusing on Quadrant 1 tasks and scheduling Quadrant 2 tasks, you ensure that you're always working on tasks that align with your goals and contribute to your influence

- **Reduced Procrastination:** The matrix forces you to confront tasks that you might have been avoiding, ensuring that nothing important gets left behind

- **Delegation and Efficiency:** By identifying tasks that can be delegated (Quadrant 3), you can free up your time and mental bandwidth for more significant endeavors

- **Elimination of Time-Wasters:** Quadrant 4 tasks often consume more time than we realize. By identifying and eliminating these tasks, you can reclaim valuable hours

How to Use the Eisenhower Matrix Effectively:

Step 1: List All Your Tasks

Begin by listing all the tasks you have on your plate. This could be anything from responding to emails and attending meetings to working on a project that aligns with your influence goals.

Step 2: Categorize the Tasks

Place each task into one of the four quadrants based on its urgency and importance:

- **Quadrant 1 (Urgent and Important):** These are tasks that require immediate attention and align with your goals
- **Quadrant 2 (Important but Not Urgent):** These are tasks that are important but don't require immediate action
- **Quadrant 3 (Urgent but Not Important):** These tasks require immediate attention but don't necessarily align with your goals
- **Quadrant 4 (Neither Urgent nor Important):** These are tasks that neither require immediate attention nor align with your goals

Step 3: Prioritize and Plan

- **Quadrant 1:** Tackle these tasks first. They are both urgent and important
- **Quadrant 2:** Schedule these tasks. They are important for your long-term goals and should not be neglected
- **Quadrant 3:** Consider delegating these tasks. They are urgent but not important to your personal goals
- **Quadrant 4:** Eliminate or minimize time spent on these tasks as they don't contribute to your goals

TIME MANAGEMENT

The Eisenhower Decision Matrix

Step 4: Review and Adjust

At the end of each week, review your matrix. Move tasks between quadrants if their urgency or importance has changed. This is also a good time to reflect on how well you're aligning your time and tasks with your influence goals.

Step 5: Integrate with Other Tools and Strategies

The Eisenhower Matrix isn't meant to be used in isolation. Integrate it with other productivity tools and strategies like the Pareto Principle Funnel for maximum effectiveness. For instance, you could use the matrix to first categorize tasks and then apply the Pareto Principle to focus on the 20% that will yield 80% of the results.

Integrating the Eisenhower Matrix with Your Influence Strategy:

- **Align with Key Influencers:** As you connect with key influencers and figures, use the matrix to prioritize collaborative projects and initiatives. This ensures that you're always working on partnerships that have the highest potential for impact.

- **Focus on High-Impact Activities:** Use the matrix in conjunction with the Pareto Principle Funnel. This combination can help you identify tasks that not only yield the most results but are also of the highest importance and urgency.

- **Empower Your Inner Hero:** As you embrace your inner hero, the matrix can guide you in choosing battles that are worth fighting. It ensures that you're always on the path of maximum impact and influence.

Assignment: Mastering the Eisenhower Matrix for Transformative Impact

- **Quadrant 1 (Urgent and Important)**: Identify at least three tasks in this quadrant that are both urgent and crucial to your influence goals. Complete these tasks immediately within the next 24-48 hours

- **Quadrant 2 (Important but Not Urgent)**: Choose two tasks that are important but not urgent. Schedule time in your calendar to complete these tasks within the next week. These should be tasks that align with your long-term goals and will have a lasting impact

- **Quadrant 3 (Urgent but Not Important)**: List down tasks that often interrupt your day but aren't crucial to your goals. Identify at least one task you can delegate to someone else or set a specific time to address these so they don't interrupt more important work

- **Quadrant 4 (Neither Urgent nor Important)**: Identify at least two tasks that you spend time on but don't contribute to your goals. Make a conscious decision to eliminate or significantly reduce time spent on these tasks

- **Reflection and Adjustment**: At the end of the week, review your matrix. Reflect on how well you were able to stick to your plan and what impact it had on your productivity and influence. Make necessary adjustments for the following week

- **Integration**: As an extra step, integrate your Eisenhower Matrix with the Pareto Principle Funnel. Identify which tasks in Quadrant 1 and 2 fall into the top 20% of activities that will yield 80% of your desired results. Prioritize these in the coming week

By completing this assignment, you'll not only become proficient in using the Eisenhower Matrix but also make strides in amplifying your influence and impact.

5. Leveraging the Power of AI for Accelerated Impact

AI offers a practical way to supercharge your influence and impact. Here's how:

- **Connecting with Key Influencers and Admired Figures**: Use AI to help you brainstorm and strategize ways to connect with key influencers and figures you admire. Input their public profiles, articles, or interviews into an AI tool and ask for insights on common interests, potential collaboration ideas, or even conversation starters.

- **Optimize Time Management**: Enter your list of weekly activities and goals into an AI-based planner. Use the planner to integrate both the Pareto Principle and the Eisenhower Matrix, helping you focus on high-impact activities that are both urgent and important.

- **Enhance Decision-Making**: Use AI as a sounding board for your ideas and decisions. Whether you're choosing a project to initiate or identifying the most impactful way to contribute to a cause, AI can provide valuable perspectives and alternatives.

- **Content Creation**: AI can assist you in drafting various types of content. Input your topic and target audience, and ask the AI to generate drafts or outlines for different formats like articles, social media posts, or even video scripts.

Assignment: Use AI to create a comprehensive battle plan that includes:

- A strategy for connecting with at least 5-10 key influencers or admired figures

- A plan for connecting with your ideal customers

- A time management plan for the upcoming week, integrating the Pareto Principle and the Eisenhower Matrix

- At least five pieces of content aimed at enhancing your influence, including a script for a video, a blog post, a social media post, an idea for an interactive social media engagement, and an email newsletter

Conclusion: The Legacy of Positive Change

You have embarked on a transformative journey, one that began by embracing the hero within you. You have recognized your immeasurable worth and envisioned a future where your influence reverberates through relationships, communities, and beyond.

From there, you have also learned to connect authentically with key influencers and admired figures, not as stepping stones, but as partners in a shared vision. You have delved into the power of focused effort through the Pareto Principle Funnel, and you have mastered the art of productivity with the Eisenhower Matrix. Finally, you have harnessed the groundbreaking capabilities of AI to supercharge every facet of your influence and impact.

This isn't just about you; it's about the world that awaits your greatness. It's about the lives you'll touch, the changes you'll inspire, and the legacy of positive change you'll leave behind. You're not just amplifying your influence; you're becoming a beacon of hope, a catalyst for change, and a true hero in your own right.

Congratulations on completing this transformative chapter. The journey doesn't end here. To further accelerate your influence and gain deeper insights, I invite you to visit http://www.impactaccelerator.ai/activate. Here, you'll receive a free PDF download and gain exclusive access to a mini-course designed to supercharge your influence.

Thank you for taking this journey with me. The world doesn't just await your greatness; it desperately needs it. So go forth and embrace your destiny.

Ian Griffith

Empowering Minds through AI and Innovation

Location: Orange County, California

Qualifications and Services:

- Speaker: Engaging audiences worldwide on topics related to Artificial Intelligence, personal development, and transformative leadership.
- Coach: Providing personalized guidance and strategies to help individuals and organizations harness the power of AI and achieve their full potential.
- Author: Sharing insights and expertise through written works, contributing to the broader discourse on AI and personal growth.
- Mastermind Leader: Facilitating dynamic mastermind groups, fostering collaborative learning, and driving innovation in the field of AI.

Connect with Ian:

- Website: www.iancgriffith.com

- Facebook: IanCGriffith
- Instagram: @iancgriffith

Ian Griffith is a renowned expert in artificial intelligence, technology, and personal development, with over two decades of experience at the forefront of innovation and education. His journey began in the tech industry, contributing significantly to internal automation and AI programs at major corporations like Intel/SAP and IBM. Recognizing his unique ability to distill complex subjects into accessible knowledge, Ian transitioned into the world of online education, establishing himself as a transformative educator and speaker.

As the founder of Impact Mastery LLC, Ian is on a mission to empower individuals and organizations to fully leverage the capabilities of AI and technology. His innovative approach to education has made him a sought-after speaker, regularly addressing groups of 500 or more, and demystifying the complexities of AI to make it accessible to a broader audience.

Ian's expertise in Generative AI and Automation has positioned him as a world authority in these domains, helping people to accelerate their impact and achieve results at an unprecedented scale. His mastermind program, TheMastermind.AI, and his course, The Mastermind Blueprint.AI, are meticulously designed to equip participants with the necessary tools and knowledge to navigate the intricate world of AI, fostering growth, accountability, and community.

A prolific author, Ian has contributed to all four volumes of the "Activate Your Life" series, sharing his insights and wisdom to inspire and guide readers on their journeys toward personal and professional excellence.

Ian also leads the Facebook Group "Accelerate Your Impact," a thriving community of 13,000 members dedicated to embracing their potential and wielding influence with confidence.

Connect with Ian through his various programs, social media platforms, and his website: www.iancgriffith.com, and embark on a journey of transformation, empowerment, and mastery in the world of AI, Generative AI, and Automation.

PART 5

RELATIONSHIP TO INNER GOALS AND OUTER ENVIRONMENT

DROP IN AND FEEL: A TOOL TO SUPPORT THE CULTIVATION OF GROUNDEDNESS AND EMBODIED PRESENCE

by Katie Snyder

What does it do?

Invites one to drop into one's body to feel whatever is present and to express in whatever way feels most supportive. I use this process at the start of almost every client session to help them to come into presence, and welcome whatever wants to be there for our session that day. This process repeated in our 1:1 work also supports a client's ability to bring themselves into presence and ground in their daily lives. The experience of this process creates an energetic bookmark that the body easily remembers after time.

Who is it useful for? Everyone! This exercise is a beautiful tool to support the cultivation of grounded and embodied presence, fostering the ability to check in with and listen to the self through the vehicle of the body. Culturally, we have gotten used to operating from the realms of the mind rather than letting the body lead the way. This exercise, which can be done solo or in a partner/group format, fosters an increased ability to listen and respond to the messages the body is relaying; thereby, with continued practice, cultivating deeper trust and more clear communication with the body.

This practice is especially impactful for supporting embodied presence through increasing one's ability to welcome and "be with" whatever is present in the body; be that felt discomfort, pain, tension, tightness as well as openness, fluidity, ease, &/or subtle energies moving throughout the body. Repeated experiences of this process thereby opens one's window of tolerance wider and wider to expand one's capacity to better feel and express what is present in the body.

When first introducing this process to a client, I guide them through the grounding process as follows. First, invite the client to find a comfortable seat in an open body position: if seated in a chair, legs and arms are uncrossed with feet firmly planted on the floor. Hands can be face down on the legs to invite more grounding or open towards the ceiling to invite receptivity. Easy pose can be taken if seated on the floor, and a folded up blanket or cushion under the sit bones can be supportive, to raise the hips above the knees and decrease strain on the low back.

If it feels right, soften the eyes down or welcome a soft gaze. As the body lands, welcome any wiggles that the body is asking for. Ask oneself, how does my body want to move? Allow intuitive guidance to come through the body and invite one's presence to drop a little deeper as you begin to welcome a deep drink of the breath in through the nose. Call that breath deep down into the belly and sigh outwardly with your exhale. Some examples of movement include:

Rotating the head side to side or drawing circles with the nose.

Rolling through the shoulders and/or squeezing the shoulders up by the ears and releasing in tandem with the breath.

Drawing circles with the spine in both directions: inhaling to the front of the circle, exhaling to the back (as if stirring the bowl of the pelvis with the spoon of the spine)

Finding stillness as you're ready, and calling forth more presence with the breath. We take around 10-15 breaths using the following technique:

Calling the breath deep down into the belly, feel the belly rise, as if you could fill the whole pelvic bowl with the breath, and exhale, sighing the breath out. The exhale can be embellished with sound (starting from a high tone and de-escalating to a lower tone welcomes one's consciousness to reach deeper into the lower chakras of the body), fluttering of the lips to release erratic energy, or whatever wants to escape from the mouth. *Sighing is a sound of pleasure and welcomes a signification of safety to the body, as the body primarily experiences pleasure from a state of embodied safety

It can be supportive to invite bright, white, sparking light to enter the body with the breath on the inhale, and black smoke leaving the mouth though the exhale, releasing stress and chaos. The inhale welcomes sparkling white light to fill the body with the breath, breathing all the way down to the pelvic floor. While the exhale delivers the breath through the pelvic floor and the feet, sending excess energy into the ground beneath you. Bringing awareness to the pelvic floor brings our consciousness into the base chakra, or the root, welcoming a felt-sense of safety into the body.

Amidst these breaths, cues are given to welcome any arising sensations the body is offering, and it is encouraged to breathe into whatever is arising, breathing into the highest sensation. It may be supportive to place the hands on the part of the body that is speaking, signifying to the body "I am here, I am listening" and offering a comforting, soothing touch.

With the final breath, calling the deepest drink of the breath in yet, and holding at the top, take another little sip of air in. From this space, the client is asked to welcome an intention they have for the session. It can be supportive to place one's hands over the heart or take a prayer position with both palms together and thumbs toward the sternum. The client holds the breath for as long as feels right, dancing with the edge of chaos between the breaths whilst welcoming the penetration of their intention deeper into the body. The exhale can be released with power, sound; maybe a shake of the body, or with softness and ease, whatever feels right in the moment.

When it feels right, find a neutral breath and allow the body to breathe itself whilst maintaining your internal gaze. From here, we flow into the space of the "feeler", welcoming expression of whatever wants to be here.

This might include:

- Verbal dump to purge/vent the mind's thoughts
- Describing sensations in the body as they arise, move, and dissipate - perhaps dialoguing with whatever is present as it shows up/moves
- Movement
- Continued deep breathing helps to turn the volume up on parts of the body that may be calling for attention. Keep breathing into the highest sensation
- Silence
- Sounds /vocalizations
- Expression of emotion is most welcomed: crying,

laughter, shouting, screaming (with the cue of alert to the one holding space that it may get loud)

- Sometimes the body has a response to the intention that was made and it can be impactful to breathe into that space and express in whatever way feels most resonant

During the space of the feeler, the one holding the space sets a timer for 2-3 minutes (I prefer 3), and holds a space of loving witness through deep listening (while the space holder is also in an open body position, signifying open readiness to receive). No reflection is given during this space, though sporadic sounds like "mm" can support the client in feeling that they are being heard, although not swayed with reflection of any kind.

A lot of information can come through this experience for both the client and coach. I often find that clients who tend to be very wordy, really drink in the silence that is offered in this space, and end up not expressing a word. It's also often the case that whatever one originally anticipated covering in the session, is usurped by something that's residing underneath and arises in this space.

After the 3 minutes are complete, the space holder asks if the client would like an additional 1-2 minutes. If yes, the timer is adjusted accordingly and we drop back in. If the client feels complete, the coach helps to guide the client back into everyday life by orienting to their space before coming back to screen/face-to-face presence. Orientation is done by scanning one's environment and landing one's focus on at least 3 objects in the environment, either saying aloud or mentally labeling such items. A "pop-out question" can also be used to support them in orientation. This is a random and simple question, such as "What is your favorite animal?" This type of question turns on the conscious mind and helps support the client in returning to the here and now.

If desired, the client can then swap spaces with the coach to practice holding space in loving witness. This helps to decrease the urge to "fix" another's experience due to our own discomfort of feeling and hearing their experience. We get to practice neutral acceptance and witness of another without any expectations of result, nor the taking on of another's energy/experience.

As the client gets used to this practice with repeated guidance and experiences, it becomes easy for them to call upon this space in times of nervous system activation/ dis-regulation in their everyday lives, increasing their sense of autonomy and self-agency in calling the self back into a state of regulation.

This practice cultivates a deep connection with self, while also releasing the fear of being seen in our fullness and authenticity. If done in a dyad format where two people take turns holding space for one another, it supports a deeper connection in intimacy with another, allowing for the embodied knowing that it is safe to share how one is feeling with someone else, through loving receptivity.

This practice is also very supportive of conflict mediation, as it creates a container for being heard as well as deeply listening to the other without interruption.

Katie Snyder

Let go. Unfurl. All of you are welcome here.

www.katiesunflower.com

@katiesunflowersnyder

www.facebook.com/tara.devpriya

Katie is a trauma-informed embodiment guide specializing in yoga, breathwork, massage therapy, meditation, reiki, yoga nidra, kundalini yoga, and sound healing. She has received extensive training and mentorship in trauma-informed leadership, deepening her skills as a transformational coach, and enjoys weaving all of her studies and experiences into curated sessions for her clients to support their continued unfurling.

Katie is impassioned in the art of gathering and loves to call together collaborative efforts for retreats, events, and monthly/weekly circles to support depth of connection.

It is Katie's ultimate wish and intention that each individual has the felt-sense experience of safety, peace and home in one's body, mind and heart. Her offerings include private sessions, classes, workshops, events and retreats in addition to 1:1 and group containers, locally and online.

GET ALIGNED & ATTRACT WEALTH, HEALTH AND LOVE, WITH INTERIOR DESIGN

by Mary Ann Benoit

What it Does

Embracing your authentic self is the cornerstone to manifesting happiness, well-being, wealth, health, and love in your life. When you genuinely align with your true self, you not only find joy in your work but also amplify its impact, drawing others to recognize your authenticity and trust in your offerings.

Authenticity paves the way for optimal health, guiding you on a journey of self-care and self-integrity.

True self-alignment attracts individuals who resonate with your essence, cultivating nourishing and supportive relationships.

Everything is energy and is interconnected, from our personal spaces to our wealth and relationships. By enhancing the energy in our living and working environments, we promote personal alignment and become magnets for health, wealth, and love.

These exercises use Aligned Design©, an innovative Interior Design philosophy, which merges art, science, and energy to create transformative spaces that support us. By harmonizing our environments with our authentic selves, we establish a foundation that uplifts and empowers us to realize our full potential. This alignment not only creates beautiful spaces, but also resonates, uplifts, and nurtures our genuine identities.

Who is It Useful For?

These two self-assessments offer immediate clarity and feedback to everyone who wants to become more aligned with their true purpose in life and wishes to attract more well-being, wealth, health, and love. The feedback helps identify personal actions and ideas to enhance our living or workspace to support us. Revisit every six months, and as you evolve, adjust your surroundings to match your growing alignment.

Both exercises total 65 minutes, but more time can be spent if desired. Exercises can be done together or spread out over time. Exercise 1 should be done first.

Exercise 1: Are You and Your Space Aligned with Who You Truly Are? (35 mins)

Objective: Determine if you're aligned with your life's purpose and assess whether your daily actions and environment support this alignment. Identify ways to optimize alignment. - 50 minutes.

Part 1: Your Alignment Assessment (10 mins)

- In a quiet spot, take 8 deep breaths in and out slowly. Allow yourself to feel open to energy above, below and surrounding you.
- Meditate on your life's purpose. Trust whatever comes to you. Journal your thoughts without judgment. Let your consciousness flow and resist editing your words. This is for your eyes only.
  - ◊ What makes you feel most alive?
  - ◊ What activities or tasks seem to resonate most with your core?
  - ◊ What makes you happy and is something you

would do even if you were never paid for it? What allows you to lose all sense of time?

Revisiting this exercise periodically allows you to adapt to changes as you continue your journey of self-discovery.

Part 2: Your Daily Activity Assessment (10 mins)

- List three actions or tasks you did today
- For each action/task, rate on a scale from 1-10 how closely it aligns with your stated life purpose (10 being fully aligned)
- Look at your ratings. If any are below an 8, write down what you believe caused the misalignment
- For each misaligned task, brainstorm how it could be changed to better align with your purpose
- What's missing, or feels out of sync?

Our daily routines are made up of small, recurring actions, shaping our habits, which in turn create our lives. Minor shifts in these routines can lead to significant life transformations. For example, I've cultivated a morning ritual where I light candles, savor fresh flowers I've bought for myself, and embrace time for silence and reflection. This practice not only boosts my well-being and creativity but also fortifies my alignment with my purpose to enrich others' lives through art and design.

Part 3: Your Space Assessment (15 mins)

Evaluate a primary room in your home or workspace. If you wish for more comprehensive insights, consider assessing additional rooms. Go with your initial feeling and avoid over-analyzing.

1. How does the room feel? Sit quietly, relax, breathe, and trust what comes to you.
   - Note how you feel emotionally and physically.

Do you feel positive? Inspired? Relaxed? Energized? Does it feel heavy, empty, depressing, or irritating?

- Note how you feel physically. Does it give you a headache or make you cough or sneeze? Does it feel comfortable or uncomfortable?

- Does it resonate with who you truly are or seem to reflect someone else?

- Do you have so many things in the room that it is difficult to do this exercise? Does it feel chaotic?

2. How do the items in the room make you feel? List the items in the room that bring you joy, inspiration, or a sense of calm. List items that evoke negative feelings or seem out of place.

3. How do the colors make you feel? List the colors that feel positive or negative to you and why.

4. How do the materials make you feel? Are most items in your space made from natural or man-made materials? Compare how natural materials make you feel versus synthetic ones. Which materials are you drawn to touch and which would you rather not engage with?

5. How does the room smell? Assess the room's aroma. Identify sources of pleasant and unpleasant scents.

6. How does the room sound? Evaluate the room's acoustics. Is it serene or filled with distractions? Identify internal or external sources of noise. Consider if these sounds disrupt activities like reading, working, or resting in this space.

Decluttering can dramatically calm and refresh a space's energy. This exercise helps you identify areas for improvement, such as adding energy art, which captures invisible forces using colors, patterns, and symbols, infused with the artist's spiritual intent. It resonates with viewers, elevating and drawing parallel energies, guiding them towards alignment and their peak potential. Other improvements could include opting for natural materials, adjusting paint colors, reducing noise, and enhancing sensory experiences through touch, sound, and scent.

Exercise 2: Elevate Your Space to Attract More Wealth, Health, and Love with Aligned Design© (30 mins)

What it Does: Once you've recognized and embraced your authentic self and cultivated a space free from negative influences on your well-being, you've laid the foundation that empowers you to reach your highest potential. This is where Aligned Design's synergy of the beauty of art, the science of color, and the energy of well-being come into play. With this solid foundation, you're poised to enhance your space, elevating your surroundings to energetically attract more wealth, health, and love into your life.

Who is it Useful For? It is useful for anyone who wants to attract more wealth, health, and love into their life by giving instant clarification and feedback on areas that can be improved through personal actions and enhancing your space. Complete this exercise after advancing with the personal alignment steps in Exercise 1. 25 minutes.

Part 1: Self-Assessment Exercise: How Are You Doing Now at Attracting Wealth, Health, and Love? (5 mins)

How are you honestly doing now at attracting wealth, health, and love into your life? For each category, rate yourself on a scale of 1-10, where 1 is "not at all" and 10 is "completely agree."

Scores below 8 show opportunities to improve personal actions and optimize your space to attract more wealth, health, and love.

Part 2- Space Assessment: Is It Attracting Wealth, Health, and Love? (25 mins)

Set Your Intention. Find a peaceful spot. Close your eyes and breathe deeply. Can you visualize your life abundant with wealth, health, and love? Now assess a main room in your home or your workspace – 5 mins

1. Wealth: (5 mins)

   - Belongings: Do you see items you no longer need? Clutter can block the flow of prosperity

   - Symbols of Success: Is there energy art to attract abundance, or items, or decor that symbolize success and abundance for you?

   - Workspace: Is your workspace tidy, functional, comfortable, and inspiring? A productive workspace can help attract financial success

   - Color: Are there wealth-associated colors such as gold, green, purple, or dark blue, in your décor? Are there specific colors you associate with wealth?

2. Health: (5 Mins)

   - Air & Light: Does your space get adequate fresh air and natural light?

   - Space Layout: Can you move freely in your space, or does it feel cramped?

   - Kitchen: Does your kitchen invite you to cook healthy meals?

   - Natural elements: Are your furniture and accessories made from natural materials? Do you have supportive high-energy items, such as energy art, crystals, flowers, and plants in your space?

- Color: Are there soothing blues or greens or colors that feel calming to you in your relaxation zones?

3. Love: (5 Mins)

- Personal Space: Are your personal areas comfortable for solo or shared moments?

- Symbols of Love: Do you have energy art or items on display that represent love or cherished memories?

- Open Spaces: Is there a welcoming shared space in your home?

- Color: Do your intimate spaces evoke feelings of warmth and coziness with colors like reds, pinks, warm neutrals, muted purples, or deep blues?

4. Reflection: (5 mins)

- Which areas feel in alignment with your goals, and which areas seem out of sync?

- Planning (5 mins)

- For areas needing change, can you list an action step for each?

Your environment plays a pivotal role in influencing your mood, actions, and energy. By ensuring your space supports your desires, you align yourself to attract more wealth, health, and love. Even minor adjustments in a space, such as decluttering or showcasing small symbols of wealth, health, and love, can make a meaningful impact.

These exercises help you update your space to enhance your personal alignment with your authentic self. This in turn will support you in attracting more happiness, well-being, wealth, health, and love into your life.

Example Transformation: I recently took a critical look at my combined living room/kitchen in my home, a central space for myself, and my Bed and Breakfast guests. My intention? An updated, authentic reflection of my present self that delights both me and my guests, showcasing my artistry and hospitality.

Wealth Assessment: Despite being tidy, the space lacked the modern touch and artistic energy, synonymous with wealth. My artist's touch was notably absent, with no energy art displayed. The primary yellow and red tones failed to convey opulence.

Health Assessment: While the room benefited from good ventilation and lighting, the kitchen's clutter and dominating red discouraged me from crafting nourishing meals. The space also lacked nature-inspired colors and materials, vital for a holistic environment.

Love Assessment: Comfortable furniture adorned the area, and personal keepsakes from travels and friends added sentiment. The kitchen's red hues did inspire a sense of warmth and togetherness.

Planning: Realizing the discord between my spaces and my current self, I mapped out steps to bridge the gap:

1. Clear out clutter
2. Infuse rooms with meaningful energy art, reflecting my current journey
3. Update color palettes to complement the chosen art
4. Refresh decor, like rugs and accessories, to match the art and new hues

Results: The area now features artwork from my "Stories of the Future" collection, steeped in blues, greens and purples. Beyond their beauty, they serve as a reminder and inspiration to reflect on, and if needed, recalibrate my life's narratives. The kitchen walls now wear a soft blue, and new rugs in blues and purples elevate both rooms. The transformation isn't just visual; it's experiential. I now love my rejuvenated kitchen and spend more time creating healthy meals. I am more inclined to invite friends over. Guest reviews often highlight the captivating art and refreshed ambience, with many expressing interest in my showcased art. The assessment and actions helped me enhance wealth, health and love in my own life.

Mary Ann Benoit

Interior Designer/Energy Artist. The Visionary Behind Aligned Design ©

Connect: Northern Lights Staging

Email: info@northernlightsstaging.com

Energy Art Collection: Pixels.com

YouTube-Saturday Night Live Art Shows

Location: Alaska

Mary Ann Benoit, President of Northern Lights Home Staging

and Design, has revolutionized the world of Interior Design, Virtual Design and Energy Art with her unique Aligned Design© system, which has a foundation in her subliminal energy art. With accolades to her name, she's renowned for her unique transformative approach to Interior Design.

Her Interior Designs are not just about aesthetics; they create magic by intertwining art, science, and energy with a foundation built on energy. She sculpts spaces that resonate with and support their inhabitants to be aligned with who they truly are. Her ethos? "When your space is better, you are better. When you are better, the world is better. And the world needs you". Her style? "Globally inspired, soulfully aligned." Using the lively color spectrum of global styles, combined with her energy-infused AI and fractal art collages with subliminal energy messages, Mary Ann's designs are more than just visually appealing; they're a testament to one's spirit and they uplift and support you to reach your highest potential.

Drawing inspiration from her 30-year tenure as a wildlife biologist, nature's splendor is intricately woven into her designs. As Alaska's exclusive Certified Color Strategist, she delivers extraordinary color using color science. Her energy art, rooted in sacred geometry, serves as a design foundation, resonating deeply with its beholders through supportive energy messages coming through layers of energy-infused fractal art. Dive into her world with an Aligned Design consultation, which includes your personalized energy art portrait. Through virtual design, she can work with you anywhere in the world. For art aficionados, her creations are available on Pixels.com and other platforms.

THE POWER OF AUTHENTIC FRAMING IN COMMUNICATION

by Rachel Gladstone

Introduction:

Effective communication is a vital component of personal and professional relationships. Whether it is in friendships, romantic relationships, or within the workplace, communicating effectively enables individuals to understand and convey their thoughts, emotions, and needs, which in turn cultivates trust, empathy, and collaboration.

In personal relationships, effective communication plays a crucial role in developing and maintaining strong connections. It allows individuals to express their emotions and concerns honestly, promoting understanding and empathy between partners or friends. When people are open and attentive listeners, conflicts can be resolved with greater ease, misunderstandings can be clarified, and compromises can be reached. Effective communication also encourages intimacy and fosters a sense of emotional security, making relationships more fulfilling and lasting.

In professional settings, effective communication is essential for building strong working alliances and achieving common goals. Clear and concise communication ensures that team members are well-informed about tasks, expectations, and deadlines, minimizing errors and enhancing productivity. Moreover, effective communication leads to a positive work environment where everyone feels respected and valued. It promotes open feedback, encourages innovation, and enables individuals to express their ideas and concerns freely. This not only improves problem-solving and decision-making processes, but also enhances employee satisfaction and morale.

Additionally, effective communication helps individuals develop stronger negotiating and conflict resolution skills. Through effective communication, different perspectives and opinions can be shared and understood, leading to finding common ground and creating win-win solutions. In both personal and professional relationships, effective communication fosters mutual understanding, respect, and collaboration, enabling people to overcome challenges and experience greater personal growth and success.

Furthermore, effective communication is crucial for establishing and maintaining trust. When individuals communicate honestly and transparently, trust is built, and relationships flourish. Trust is the foundation of any successful relationship and without it, both personal and professional relationships can suffer. By communicating effectively, individuals demonstrate integrity, reliability, and dependability, instilling confidence and strengthening the bonds between them.

Effective communication is an indispensable aspect of personal and professional relationships. It facilitates understanding, empathy, collaboration, and trust, enabling individuals to build strong connections, resolve conflicts, and achieve common goals. By prioritizing effective communication, individuals can establish rewarding and lasting relationships, both personally and professionally.

Authentic framing is a powerful tool to enhance communication, fostering genuine and meaningful interactions in personal and professional relationships. It involves presenting information, ideas, and perspectives in a sincere and authentic manner, promoting openness, trust, and understanding.

In a world where communication often involves polished presentations and carefully crafted messages, authentic framing encourages individuals to communicate in a way that aligns with their true selves. It goes beyond simply delivering information and instead aims to create a connection by sharing thoughts, experiences, and emotions sincerely.

Authentic framing values honesty and vulnerability, allowing individuals to express their true thoughts and feelings without fear of judgment, or reprisal. By embracing authenticity, communication becomes more genuine, creating space for deeper connections to form.

Authentic framing also invites active listening, where individuals not only hear what is being said, but also strive to understand the underlying emotions and motivations behind the words. By truly engaging with others and empathetically responding to their authentic framing, individuals can build stronger and more empathetic relationships.

This approach to communication also encourages individuals to be mindful of their non-verbal cues, such as body language and facial expressions, which can communicate additional meaning and authenticity. By aligning verbal and non-verbal communication, individuals can reinforce the sincerity of their message and create a more impactful connection with their audience.

Authentic framing is particularly beneficial in resolving conflicts, as it promotes honesty, empathy, and understanding. By openly sharing perspectives and listening without judgment, individuals can work towards finding mutually beneficial resolutions that address the needs and concerns of all parties involved.

In summary, authentic framing is a powerful tool for enhancing communication in both personal and professional relationships. By embracing authenticity, individuals can foster genuine connections, trust, and understanding. It encourages active listening, empathy, and the alignment of verbal and non-verbal communication. Incorporating authentic framing into our interactions can lead to more fulfilling relationships and more effective communication overall.

Section 1: Understanding Authentic Framing

Authentic framing can be defined as the practice of expressing thoughts and emotions honestly and transparently in conversations. It involves communicating in a manner that reflects your genuine beliefs, values, and experiences, while being mindful of the impact your words may have on others. It emphasizes sincerity, transparency, and a commitment to open and genuine communication. By engaging in authentic framing, you aim to foster trust, establish meaningful connections, and promote understanding in your conversations.

Section 2: Applying Authentic Framing in Communication

Authentic framing in everyday conversations involves expressing your true thoughts and feelings, while considering the impact of your words on others. It is about being genuine, respectful, and empathetic in your communication. Here are some practical tips for applying authentic framing in your everyday conversations:

1. **Reflect on Your Intentions**: Before starting a conversation, be clear about your intentions. Ask yourself why you are initiating this conversation and what outcome or connection you hope to achieve. Authentic framing requires genuine motives and a sincere desire for mutual understanding.

2. **Be Mindful of Your Words**: Pay attention to the words you choose and the tone of your voice. Use language that is honest and respectful, avoiding exaggerated or misleading statements. Aim for clarity and simplicity, expressing your thoughts in a way that is easily understood by others.

3. **Practice Active Listening**: Authentic framing involves not only expressing yourself but also actively listening to others. Show genuine interest in what the other person is saying, maintain eye contact, and avoid interrupting. This demonstrates respect and creates a space for open and honest dialogue.

4. **Speak from the Heart**: When expressing your own thoughts and feelings, be authentic and sincere. Share your opinions honestly, but also be aware of how your words may impact others. Choose your words carefully, balancing honesty with kindness and empathy.

5. **Empathize with Others**: Authentic framing also requires putting yourself in the shoes of the person you are speaking with. Try to understand their perspective and feelings, even if you don't agree with them. This helps create a sense of connection and mutual respect, fostering meaningful conversations.

6. **Avoid Judging or Blaming**: Instead of assigning blame or passing judgment, focus on expressing your

own experiences and emotions. Use "I" statements to express your thoughts and feelings without making the other person defensive. This encourages a more open and non-confrontational dialogue.

7. **Be Open to Different Perspectives**: Authentic framing involves being open-minded and willing to consider different viewpoints. Even if you strongly disagree with someone, try to understand their perspective and engage in a respectful discussion. This can lead to a more enriching and inclusive conversation.

8. **Seek Common Ground**: Look for shared interests, values, or goals to build a sense of connection and understanding. Finding common ground helps create a more collaborative and constructive conversation, where both parties feel heard and respected.

9. **Practice Emotional Awareness**: Being aware of your emotions and how they influence your communication is crucial for authentic framing. Take a moment to identify your emotions before engaging in a conversation, and be mindful of how they may impact your words. If needed, take a break or ask for clarification if emotions start to escalate.

10. **Practice Self-Reflection**: Regularly reflect on your communication style and the impact it has on others. Consider seeking feedback from trusted friends or colleagues to gain insights into how well you are applying authentic framing. Use this feedback to improve and grow in your communication skills.

Remember, authentic framing is a continuous process of growth and learning. By practicing these tips, you can enhance your everyday conversations, foster deeper connections, and promote understanding and respect in your interactions with others.

Here are some practical tips for applying authentic framing in everyday conversations:

1. **Self-awareness**: Start by being aware of your thoughts, emotions, beliefs, and values. Understand yourself and how you truly feel about a particular topic before entering a conversation.

2. **Practice active listening**: Give your full attention to the person speaking, demonstrating that you value their thoughts and feelings. Focus on understanding their perspective without interrupting or formulating a response in your mind.

3. **Be honest and transparent**: Express your thoughts and emotions truthfully, while being mindful of how you convey them. Avoid exaggerating or withholding information. Strive for clarity and sincerity in your communication.

4. **Use "I" statements**: When expressing your opinions or feelings, use "I" statements to take ownership of your thoughts and emotions. For example, say "I feel" or "I believe" instead of making generalized statements.

5. **Respect differing perspectives**: Acknowledge and respect that others may have different viewpoints or experiences. Be open to understanding their point of view and avoid judgment or defensiveness.

6. **Embrace vulnerability**: Being authentic means having the courage to share your thoughts, even if they may be uncomfortable or unpopular. Embrace vulnerability by expressing yourself honestly, while keeping the conversation constructive and respectful.

7. **Seek understanding**: When engaging in discussions, prioritize understanding over winning arguments. Ask

open-ended questions, seek clarification, and show genuine curiosity about the other person's viewpoint.

8. Reflect on your communication: Take time to reflect on your conversations and interactions. Consider whether you effectively expressed your thoughts and emotions authentically. Identify areas for improvement and strive to enhance your communication skills.

9. Practice empathy: Put yourself in the shoes of the person you're conversing with and try to understand their perspective, emotions, and needs. Show empathy by validating their feelings and demonstrating compassion.

10. Be patient and compassionate: Remember that authentic framing is a continuous practice. It takes time to develop meaningful conversations and connections. Be patient with yourself and others, and approach conversations with kindness and compassion.

By incorporating these tips into your everyday interactions, you can cultivate a habit of authentic framing, creating more honest, meaningful, and fulfilling conversations.

Section 3: Communication Challenges and Solutions

Communication challenges are common in any interaction, and they can significantly impact conflict resolution and authentic framing. Here are some common challenges and strategies for overcoming them:

1. Misunderstandings:

Active listening: Give your full attention to the person speaking, and avoid distractions or assumptions. Repeat back or paraphrase what you've understood to ensure clarity.

Clarification: When in doubt, ask for clarification. Seek to understand the other person's perspective by asking specific questions about their thoughts, feelings, or statements.

Use clear and concise language: Be mindful of using jargon, ambiguous terms, or complex language. Opt for simplicity and clarity in your communication to minimize misunderstandings.

2. Defensiveness:

Practice self-awareness: Be mindful of your emotional reactions and triggers. Recognize when you start feeling defensive and take a step back to reflect before responding.

Separate facts from interpretation: Clarify the actual facts and statements being made, instead of assuming intentions or making assumptions. This helps avoid becoming defensive based on misinterpretations.

Emotional regulation: Take deep breaths, be present, and manage your emotions before responding. Responding in a calm and composed manner reduces defensiveness and fosters open dialogue.

3. Emotional barriers:

Empathy and validation: Acknowledge the other person's emotions and validate their feelings. Show understanding, compassion, and genuine concern for their experiences.

Create a safe space: Foster an environment where individuals feel comfortable expressing emotions without judgment or reprisal. Assure them that their emotions are valid and that their perspectives are valued.

Self-awareness and regulation: Understand your own emotions and take steps to regulate them. Being self-aware allows you to respond to emotions in a measured and thoughtful way, creating space for emotional connection.

4. Reflective listening:

Active listening: Give your full attention and focus on understanding the other person's perspective.

Paraphrase and summarize: Reflect back the main points, feelings, or concerns expressed by the other person. This demonstrates your attention and shows that you value their thoughts and emotions.

Non-verbal cues: Show active engagement through body language, eye contact, nodding, and appropriate facial expressions. This encourages the speaker to feel heard and understood.

5. Seeking clarification:

Open-ended questions: Ask questions that encourage the other person to elaborate and provide additional information. This helps avoid assumptions and promotes a deeper understanding.

Non-judgmental tone: Approach the other person's perspective with curiosity and a desire to understand, rather than with judgment or preconceived notions.

Avoid interruptions: Allow the other person to fully express their thoughts without interruption. Take notes if needed to address any clarifications later.

6. Practicing self-awareness:

Reflect on your own thoughts and emotions: Understand

how your emotions and beliefs may influence your communication and reactions to conflicts. Recognize your internal triggers and biases.

Take responsibility for your responses: Instead of blaming others, focus on how you can improve your communication and address any misunderstandings or defensiveness.

Seek feedback: Ask for feedback from trusted individuals on how you come across in conversations and conflicts. This can provide valuable insights for self-awareness and growth.

By implementing these strategies, you can overcome common communication challenges, promote effective dialogue, and contribute to more successful conflict resolution and authentic framing.

Section 4: Authentic Framing in Conflict Resolution

Authentic framing can play a significant role in conflict resolution. Here's how you can apply authentic framing principles specifically in conflict situations:

1. Create a safe and non-judgmental space: Foster an environment where all parties feel comfortable expressing their thoughts and emotions without fear of judgment. Encourage open communication and active listening.

2. Start with self-reflection: Before engaging in a conflict resolution conversation, take time to reflect on your own feelings and motivations. Identify any biases or preconceived notions you may have. This self-reflection helps you approach the conversation with authenticity and self-awareness.

3. Express your emotions and needs: Clearly communicate your emotions and needs related to the conflict. Use "I" statements to take responsibility for your own feelings and avoid blaming or accusing others. Be specific about what actions or changes you desire to resolve the conflict.

4. Seek to understand: Listen empathetically to the perspectives and emotions of the other party involved in the conflict. Show genuine curiosity and ask open-ended questions to gain a deeper understanding of their underlying concerns or motivations.

5. Validate emotions: Acknowledge and validate the emotions expressed by all parties involved. Recognize that emotions are a legitimate part of the conflict and that each person's feelings deserve validation and respect.

6. Find common ground: Identify shared interests or goals that both parties can agree upon. Focus on areas of mutual understanding and build upon them to establish a foundation for resolving the conflict.

7. Collaborate on solutions: Engage in a collaborative problem-solving process, where all parties actively contribute to finding a solution. Encourage brainstorming and consider multiple perspectives. Seek win-win outcomes that address the needs and concerns of all involved.

8. Be open to compromise: Recognize that finding a resolution may require some level of compromise from all parties involved. Be willing to be flexible and seek a middle ground that allows for a solution everyone can accept.

9. Practice active and empathetic listening: Give each person involved in the conflict an opportunity to speak

uninterrupted. Focus on understanding their underlying needs and concerns, rather than just responding to their words. Demonstrate empathy by acknowledging their perspective and emotions.

10. Emphasize building and maintaining relationships: Remember that conflict resolution is not just about reaching a resolution; it's also about preserving relationships. Emphasize the importance of the relationship and strive for a resolution that strengthens rather than weakens it.

By applying the principles of authentic framing in conflict resolution, you can create an atmosphere of trust, empathy, and collaboration. This approach increases the likelihood of finding mutually satisfactory resolutions while maintaining healthy relationships.

Section 5: Authentic Framing in Personal Growth

Authentic framing plays a crucial role in personal growth and self-discovery, by allowing individuals to understand and express themselves genuinely. Here's how it can contribute to personal growth:

1. Self-Awareness:

Authentic framing encourages individuals to reflect on their thoughts, feelings, and experiences. It prompts self-exploration and helps in identifying personal values, strengths, and areas for improvement. By understanding oneself better, individuals can take intentional steps towards personal growth.

2. Expression of Authenticity:

Authentic framing provides a platform for individuals

to express their true selves without fear of judgment or pretense. It encourages individuals to embrace their unique perspectives, opinions, and emotions, fostering a sense of authenticity and genuine self-expression.

3. Building Empathy and Connection:

When individuals engage in authentic framing, they open themselves up to vulnerability, allowing others to relate and connect at a deeper level. Authentic sharing of personal experiences and emotions nurtures empathy, understanding, and meaningful connections with others, promoting personal growth through interpersonal relationships.

4. Honesty and Accountability:

Authentic framing entails being honest with oneself and being accountable for one's actions and choices. It requires individuals to confront their fears, insecurities, and areas of growth while actively seeking ways to improve. This process of self-reflection and accountability promotes personal growth, and pushes individuals to strive for their best selves.

5. Embracing Vulnerability:

Vulnerability is an essential aspect of authentic framing that leads to personal growth. It involves embracing discomfort and being open about one's fears, failures, and challenges. By being vulnerable, individuals can learn from their experiences, seek support, and develop resilience, ultimately fostering personal growth and self-discovery.

6. Increased Self-Confidence:

Through authentic framing, individuals learn to embrace their true selves and develop a sense of self-confidence. When individuals have the freedom to express themselves authentically, it boosts their self-esteem and belief in their own abilities and authenticity. This self-confidence facilitates personal growth and empowers individuals to pursue their aspirations.

In conclusion, authentic framing contributes significantly to personal growth and self-discovery. It fosters self-awareness, encourages genuine self-expression, promotes empathy and connection, emphasizes honesty and accountability, embraces vulnerability, and enhances self-confidence. By engaging in authentic framing, individuals can embark on a transformative journey of personal growth and empowerment.

Section 6: Cultivating Authentic Framing in Relationships

Authentic framing is essential for building and maintaining healthy relationships. Here's how it plays a crucial role:

1. Fostering Trust and Intimacy:

Authentic framing nurtures trust within relationships by promoting open and honest communication. When individuals feel free to express themselves authentically, it creates a safe space for vulnerability and deepens the bond between individuals. Trust is the foundation for healthy relationships, and authentic framing helps to establish and strengthen that trust.

2. Establishing Emotional Connection:

Authentic framing allows individuals to share their true thoughts, feelings, and experiences without fear of judgment or rejection. This level of openness and vulnerability fosters emotional connections within relationships. When individuals authentically express themselves, it encourages the other person to reciprocate, leading to a deeper understanding and connection.

Tips for cultivating authentic framing in relationships:

In Romantic Relationships:

Practice active listening: Give your partner your full attention and genuinely listen to their thoughts and emotions without judgment.

Be open about your feelings: Share your fears, insecurities, and desires honestly, cultivating a safe space for vulnerability and emotional intimacy.

Regularly check-in: Take time to communicate about the state of the relationship, expressing any concerns or needs, authentically.

In Friendships:

Create a judgment-free zone: Establish an environment where friends can share their true selves without fear of criticism or rejection.

Encourage vulnerability: Lead by example and be open about your experiences, emotions, and challenges. This will encourage your friends to do the same.

Offer support and validation: Validate your friends' feelings and emotions, let them know that they can trust you to listen and be there for them authentically.

In Family Dynamics:

Practice active and non-judgmental listening: Provide a safe space for family members to express themselves authentically.

Choose empathy over judgment: Seek to understand each family member's perspective and emotions without criticism or dismissal.

Foster open communication: Encourage family members to share their thoughts, feelings, and concerns openly, creating an atmosphere of trust and understanding.

In all relationships, it's crucial to remember that authentic framing requires active effort from both parties. It's a mutual exchange of trust, vulnerability, and openness. By cultivating authentic framing within relationships, individuals can experience deeper connections, enhanced trust, and ultimately, a more meaningful and fulfilling relationship.

Section 7: Authentic Framing in Professional Settings

Authentic framing is not limited to personal relationships; it also has significant implications in professional settings. Here's how it can positively impact professional relationships and career success:

1. Building Trust and Rapport:

Authentic framing in professional relationships establishes trust, which is crucial for effective collaboration. When individuals communicate honestly and transparently, it fosters a sense of reliability and authenticity, leading to stronger relationships with colleagues, clients, and team members. Trust allows for increased cooperation, mutual respect, and better overall teamwork.

2. Enhancing Communication and Efficiency:

Clear and transparent communication is essential for effective collaboration. Authentic framing encourages individuals to express their thoughts, ideas, and concerns openly, leading to a better understanding among team members. This clarity minimizes misunderstandings, resolves conflicts, and increases efficiency in the workplace.

3. Encouraging Innovation and Creativity:

Authentic framing in professional settings creates an environment where individuals feel comfortable expressing their unique perspectives and ideas. This atmosphere fosters creativity and innovation, as team members can freely contribute their thoughts without fear of judgment or rejection.

Strategies for applying authentic framing in professional settings:

In Team Collaborations:

Foster an environment of psychological safety: Create a supportive environment where team members feel comfortable sharing their ideas, concerns, and feedback openly.

Encourage diverse opinions: Value different perspectives and provide opportunities for team members to contribute their unique insights without fear of judgment.

Practice active listening: Pay attention and genuinely hear others' viewpoints and suggestions, encouraging open dialogue and collaboration.

In Client Relationships:

Be transparent and honest: Establish trust with clients by providing clear and honest communication about project progress, potential challenges, and realistic expectations.

Regularly check-in: Keep the lines of communication open by regularly updating clients about the status of projects, addressing any concerns promptly, and seeking feedback to ensure satisfaction.

In Leadership Roles:

Lead by example: Demonstrate authenticity and transparency in your communication with your team. Encourage open dialogue, and be receptive to feedback and constructive criticism.

Provide constructive feedback: Deliver feedback in a respectful, honest, and supportive manner, promoting growth and improvement in team members.

Communicate goals and expectations clearly: Set clear expectations, communicate objectives, and provide regular updates, facilitating a transparent and productive work environment.

By cultivating authentic framing in professional settings, individuals can establish trust, foster effective communication, and promote a positive and collaborative work culture. This contributes to increased job satisfaction, enhanced relationships, and ultimately, career success.

Section 8: Overcoming Barriers and Nurturing Authentic Framing

Overcoming barriers and nurturing authentic framing in professional settings requires an understanding of common obstacles, and employing strategies to overcome them. Here are some key points to consider:

1. Fear of Judgment:

Fear of judgment can hinder authentic framing, as individuals may worry about how others will perceive their thoughts, ideas, or vulnerabilities. To overcome this barrier:

Develop self-acceptance: Recognize and value your own unique qualities, thoughts, and ideas. Embrace your authenticity and trust in your abilities.

Practice self-compassion: Be kind and understanding towards yourself if you make mistakes or face challenges. Treat yourself with the same understanding and empathy you would offer to others.

Seek support: Surround yourself with a supportive network of colleagues, mentors, or friends who encourage your authenticity and provide constructive feedback.

2. Social Conditioning:

Social conditioning can make it challenging for individuals to express their true selves in a professional setting. Traditional workplace norms or expectations may discourage openness or vulnerability. To overcome this barrier:

Challenge assumptions and norms: Question the validity and impact of societal and workplace norms that hinder authenticity. Advocate for a more inclusive and open work culture.

Seek role models: Find examples of individuals who authentically express themselves in professional settings. Observe how they navigate challenges and incorporate their learnings into your own approach.

Share stories and experiences: Share personal experiences that highlight the value of authenticity in professional settings. This can help shift perspectives and encourage others to be more authentic as well.

3. Tools for Overcoming Barriers:

Build self-confidence: Engage in self-reflection and self-assessment to understand your skills, strengths, and accomplishments. Develop a positive self-image and believe in your abilities.

Practice assertive communication: Learn and practice assertive communication skills to express your thoughts, needs, and opinions clearly and confidently.

Seek feedback: Regularly ask for feedback from trusted colleagues or mentors to gain insights into how you are perceived and find opportunities for growth.

Embrace vulnerability: Recognize that vulnerability is not a weakness but a strength. Accept that taking risks and being vulnerable can lead to growth and stronger connections.

4. Consistency and Practice:

Nurturing authentic framing skills requires practice and consistency:

Start small: Begin by expressing your authentic self in low-stakes situations and gradually build towards more challenging scenarios. This allows for incremental growth and increased comfort.

Reflect and learn: After interactions, take time to reflect on how effectively you expressed your authentic self and identify areas for improvement.

Seek feedback: Engage in open conversations about authenticity with colleagues or mentors, and actively seek their perspectives on your growth and progress.

Cultivate self-awareness: Regularly check in with yourself to assess how authentic you are being, in various situations. Be mindful of any barriers that may arise and work to overcome them.

Nurturing authentic framing skills takes time, patience, and perseverance. It is an ongoing process of self-discovery and growth. By addressing barriers, utilizing tools, and consistently practicing authenticity, individuals can develop a strong foundation for nurturing authentic professional relationships and achieving career success.

Rachel Gladstone

https://amzn.to/45Xm5UZ

https://www.amazon.com/author/embraceyourtrueself

https://m.facebook.com/groups/803038307145546/?ref=share&mibextid=RollTX

https://instagram.com/embrace.your.true.self?igshid=8yzuw20nlskh

Business page : Embrace Your True Self

https://www.facebook.com/EmbraceYourTrueSelf2020?mibextid=LQQJ4d

Domestic Violence, bullying & abuse help and support group on Facebook (2k members)

https://m.facebook.com/groups/803038307145546/?ref=share&mibextid=S66gvF

Phone: 248-974-7481

Location: Michigan

I'm Rachel Lynn Gladstone, and I'm proud to say I grew up in a charming village in Québec, Canada. In 1994, I embarked on a new chapter in Michigan and have been experiencing the vibrancy of the state ever since!

As a dedicated single parent, I find immense fulfillment in raising my two incredible boys, Steven and Wyatt. They hold a special place in my heart, and I believe that age should never hinder anyone from pursuing their dreams. I lead by example, encouraging my children to embrace their passions at any stage in life.

The great outdoors brings out my free-spirited nature, and you can often find me seeking solace and excitement in activities like camping, hiking, and tending to my own garden. Cooking and canning are also passions of mine, and I love creating delicious homemade meals. When I'm not exploring nature or the kitchen, I find inspiration in museums and other visual wonders, appreciating the beauty of artistic expression.

Making a positive impact on others is my unwavering commitment. I dedicate my energy to volunteering and acts of kindness. In 2020, I took the personal initiative to establish a support group for victims and survivors of domestic violence, abuse, and bullying, drawing on my own experiences to provide empathy, understanding, and guidance.

My journey has had its fair share of obstacles, but I've honed my resilience and determination along the way. Conquering bouts of anxiety and depression, I pursued various techniques and therapies to address the root causes and achieve healing. Now, as a board-certified Life & Success Coach and Clinical Hypnotherapist, I specialize in transformative techniques like EFT, NLP, and T.I.M.E., supporting others on their own paths to personal growth and well-being.

I'm also an accomplished published author, proudly featured in the esteemed compilation 'Activate Your Life, Volume Three.' This anthology brings together a renowned group of 23 inspiring life coaches from different corners of the globe, and I have contributed a captivating chapter titled 'Daily Practices for Rebuilding Self-Love.' Within this chapter, I delve into two powerful practices that have the potential to transform lives: the transformative Mirror Work and the calming Square/Box Breathing technique. Through my words, I strive to empower individuals and guide them towards a path of self-discovery and enhanced self-love. Now, let's embark on your personal journey of growth and empowerment together!"

LETTING GO OF THE PAST, EXERCISE: THE SWORD OF BABYLON

by Vikenty Mahotkin

Letting go of the past can be difficult and scary as we often get used to our dark comfort zone and grow attached to it. When we perceive multiple benefits to our present situation, it is challenging to change it. This is where the exercise, Sword of Babylon, comes in. It allows you to quickly sever ties to the past and ties to old patterns, contracts, vows, obligations, guilt and other limitations. As you hold these limitations in place, they prevent you from moving forward. Such limitations might be compared to dragging a bag of bricks and anchors behind you to make sure you don't stray too far outside the norm. Consequently, appearing to be "normal" to the people around you is perceived as allowing you to stay safe.

The truth is, you are not "normal" – you are magnificent. Your "normal" is likely very different to what society defines as the norm. Perhaps you complete tasks faster and easier than most people, even if it is right before the deadline. Perhaps you read people, rooms, and situations at a glance and in a heartbeat, and you know what everyone is feeling, thinking and even what they bring to the table; often feeling their emotions as your own. Perhaps you have more than 50 tabs open in your internet browser, covering multiple hobbies, circles of friends, and projects, all at the same time.

You may have judged yourself for doing this and NOT doing what everyone else is doing. While everyone else is perceiving only through their own eyes and minds, while totally ignoring their other senses and awareness. Through this self-imposed judgment, you may have attempted to hide your true light from the world, layering distortions, masks, and invisibility cloaks – all in an effort to cover up your light, your greatness, and your power – in order to fit in. I have come to say, no more hiding! This exercise will help you release your light into the world and shine with the brilliant luminance of who you truly are and the magic you carry.

Begin by getting centered. Get into a comfortable position (preferably sitting), then take 3 deep breaths into your heart and tune into your state right in this present moment. How are you feeling? What is your energy like? What is your body feeling? Is your mind racing?

Once you have established your current state, picture your body as if you are standing with your arms and legs spread out, with an energy bubble of dense light around you about 1 meter in diameter. What color is it? Are there multiple colors? What does it feel like to focus your attention on this bubble? What kind of awareness, thoughts, ideas, or feelings are you experiencing as you focus on the energy bubble around your body?

Now picture that you have a sword or an exacto knife, and cut through the outer shell of this bubble from the outside. First, cut into the edge of the energy bubble and go only a few centimeters deep (it is best if you actually *feel* this as you picture it).

Some notes around this so you have clarity about what is going on. You are NOT cutting into the aura or your own energy bubble as you do this. You are merely cutting away the muddy crust of beliefs, energies and cords that no longer serve you and that merely dim your light. You are not damaging your core structure - you are clearing the lens for it to shine brightly.

Often people who are highly intuitive, full of love, power, magic, kindness, and compassion (does any of this sound like *You*?) enter others' energy space and try to help them, by diving into their pool of life, their reality, their world, so that they understand what is going on and can help to heal. The trouble with this is that it is often easier to enter others' energy fields, but we are not taught to exit/disconnect. This means that you are treading water from one pool to the next, mixing energies that are not your own, so you eventually can become a cocktail of fear, doubt, depression, sabotage, fatigue and even physical illness.

The longer you are in these foreign energies, the stronger they hold on and can become like a crusty mud cake on your boots. This limits the light of your soul, magic, power, love and everything that you truly are from shining into the world. Which often leads to a decrease in energy, creativity, liveliness, happiness, love and money flows.

So what we are doing in this exercise is cutting away at these muddy crusts, to get to the juicy light of your soul that is here to shine beautifully into the world. You are not damaging your aura - you are just clearing away the dust from your light bulb so that you can shine fully and brightly.

In order to make this exercise even more effective, you may want to practice this feeling by cutting into a piece of cardboard or a plastic bottle, just to familiarize yourself with the feeling and sound, as well as the visualization.

Next, start cutting just above your left hand and move clockwise along the edge of the energy bubble, avoiding cutting directly into the body. Then, keep cutting and feeling, from left to right (cutting along the line of the energy egg 1 meter around your body, and going a few centimeters in, just like opening up a Kinder surprise. Continue cutting, being sure to stay at the edge of the energy bubble, and make your way around your entire body, going over your head, right arm, right leg, left leg, and left arm.

Once you have made a full circle, cut around the body in this way, picture and feel as you push out with your arms into the halves of the energy bubble. Like a Kinder surprise toy breaking out of its chocolate shell, feel the two halves fall away, releasing your light into the world as the two halves of the energy bubble fall in front of you and behind you, disappearing and fading away just before they hit the floor.

Take note of what happens and what it feels like to release this.

Now, let's make the second cut. Picture your new energy bubble around your body in the same spread- out position, and make note of any changes to the color and texture of the new bubble.

Begin the second cut into the energy bubble, starting behind the center of your head. As before, see and feel the incision slice the bubble (but not the body). Cut from the back of the head to the front, then down the front of the body, all the way down the front of the legs and then loop around the back of the body to the starting point at the center of the head.

Push out with your arms to the sides and feel the old energy bubble shell fall away and disappear, just before it touches the ground.

What does it feel like? Do you feel lighter, clearer, more easeful, or more peaceful?

A lady I shared this exercise with wrote to me a week after she started using it and shared amazing results. Indeed, I have received a great deal of positive feedback from people I have shared this exercise with. One woman had been judging herself for not being like her parents and family, so much so that she had taken refuge and moved to a small island in a recluse-like fashion. She started doing this exercise daily and began to experience visions as her psychic gifts flourished. She saw many past lives where she was a powerful mage, druid, cleric, healer and leader. She saw herself protecting her community from outside attacks, casting blessings, actualizing healings, and inspiring the warriors and her people as a whole.

With each vision, she realized more and more of the power she had inside, including the energy to create magic and miracles. The more this information normalized and sank into her body, the more grounded she became, leading to a feeling of calmness and sureness of herself. She realized that all her visions and dreams throughout life were not just fancies of her imagination, but rather they were her intuition, reminding her of the power within.

A week later, her entire energy field had shifted and she emerged as a new woman, radiant, calm in her power, and sure of herself and her ability to handle anything she might face in life.

Over the next month, she discovered and mastered how to talk to entities, and even had them help her manifest a new couch and a few thousand dollars. She also received clarity on how to radically change her business from a safe, logical model into something that ignited her passion and heart. She went on to launch her new business model and received her first client within just one week.

Sometimes people hold their power and magic back because of past trauma, due to not being able to save another, or because they did not take action in time to avoid a terrible incident of some sort. Please know that just because something happened in the past, it doesn't have to keep repeating in your life. You can release the past now and be free of it, free to use your power and magic to bring lightness and joy to the world, and ultimately help those you are here to help and guide them to a new tomorrow.

Let go of the weight of the past and you will no longer have to fight yourself or feel like you are pressing on the gas and brake at the same time. Allow yourself to thrive, flourish and be seen. You are here for so much more than the pain of the past.

It is time to soar and be all of you. You have the power to change the world and your own life. Allow yourself to accept this truth into your body and notice yourself feel more wonderfully and radiantly alive, vibrant and full of energy, more so than you may have felt in a long time.

Personally, I use this exercise when I feel stuck or tense, such as when I have writer's block and feel unsure of which steps to take in my life. It quickly creates lightness and relaxation, allowing me to take a fresh look at the situation without feeling trapped in tension or apprehension. This exercise allows me to clearly see which patterns of the past I am holding onto, and then make a conscious choice to do something different.

After all, doing the same thing over and over again without getting the result you want is quite insane. 😊

Wishing you all the best and lightest from the heart, as you use this exercise to make your light shine bright in the world to serve humanity and the planet.

Thank you for taking the time to read and practice this exercise.

The world is looking forward to receiving ALL of your light.

Bring it on.

Let's play.

You are worth it.

Vikentii Makhotkin

Service: Self-love and Empowerment coach

Location: Based in Ubud, Bali

Vikentii Makhotkin is a self-love and empowerment coach. He teaches people to activate the magic, power and love within, to see life through the eyes of love and truth, in order to co-create a great life for themselves while serving the entire planet as a whole ecosystem.

Since 2004, Vikentii has gathered experience with over 70 different modalities (from shamanism to theta healing, access consciousness and others) and has channeled a new one into this world – Divine Benevolence - which reminds people that we are coherent with the universe and that it wants us to succeed in our wildest desires, without thwarting ourselves and playing small. He brings this magic to the surface of everyone he works with, helping them see the world through the eyes of a God Child, enamored with life and play.

His signature offer, Soul Fire, helps you ignite your powerful authenticity in order to show up for the world in a way that is playful and sincere, serving the needs of humanity in a way that feels good and expansive, while being generously rewarded for it.

With many years of experience in IT, Vikentii brings a new spin to balanced spirituality, helping you see how everything can be thought of as a computer program, and how to delete old programs, update the software of your mind and soul, to bring about change quickly and playfully.

Born in Moscow, Russia, raised in Vancouver, Canada and currently living in Bali, Indonesia.

https://www.facebook.com/vikentiy.mahotkin

https://www.linkedin.com/in/vikentiy-mahotkin/

https://www.instagram.com/vikentiymahotkin/

THE 9 YEAR LETTER

by Ray Blakney

Imagine that in 9 years you achieve all your goals. How great would your life be? Let's take it a step further. Imagine that today, you are given a map to follow so you can reach your ideal life. This is what the 9 Year Letter™ will do for you.

A lost traveler might survey their surroundings and realize they are not where they intended to be. When you ask such an individual where they actually want to be, however, they often cannot respond with a clear answer. This is generally due to a lack of vision and clarity around what one actually wants. If this resonates, you are in the right place. Once you have completed this exercise, you will have clarified the specific and personal direction of the next season in your life AND you will be ready to embark on a defined plan to achieve it.

Great for:

- People looking to define direction and purpose for the next season of their lives
- Those who feel that their lives are not as they had hoped
- People who want a way to set a meaningful goal for their life paths and futures

---

As the baseball great Yogi Berra once said, "If you don't know where you are going, you'll end up someplace else."

The 9 Year Letter™ is an exercise that will help you establish where you want to be and how to get there. This exercise is designed around a nine-year timeframe because life is made up of different seasons. As time goes on, our dreams and goals often evolve and sometimes even change completely. A 22-year-old and a 58-year-old naturally have different visions for the time laid out before them.

Imagine yourself at the ages of 9, 18, and 27. What did you hope for? What did you dream of? Where did you want to go in life? What did you wish to achieve? How did those goals shift and develop as you experienced more of life and continued to grow as a person?

The 9 Year Letter™ will give you both a destination and a practical way to get there. When those 9 years are up and you have reached your destination, you can begin again, with a new destination designed around your desires for the next season of your life.

With this exercise, you will be well-equipped to guide others in defining their ideal destination and the steps they need to take in order to get there. Intending to arrive is not enough; you need an actionable plan.

Of course, it's important to remember that having a destination in mind does not guarantee that you will reach it, but not having a destination guarantees that you will not.

Step 1 - The Four Pillars of Your Perfect Life

Dare to Dream

Life is a road and your destination is your home. This is not just any home, this is your dream home, the place where you have everything you dreamed of for this season of your life.

Your perfect life is a house held up by four pillars. If any of those pillars are too weak, too short, or even too long, then the structure of your house will be weak. The key to a dream home is not only in the structure itself but also in the life that fills this space. It is this life that we are going to build with this part of the exercise.

For the 9 Year Letter™, the first thing you need to do is define in detail the four pillars of your dream house.

On a piece of paper, draw four columns and put the following headers at the top of each column.

1st - Family & Friends

2nd - Financial

3rd - Health

4th - Fun

Now, in each column, make a detailed list of what each of those pillars in your life will include in 9 years. The more details, the better. To get you started, here are leading questions to help you populate each column:

Family & Friends

- Describe your family members and friends in detail, especially how they make you feel
- What do you regularly do together?
- What are some memorable shared experiences?
- How does each person show up in their personal lives and how have you helped them get there?
- What are some major life events that have happened recently for your family?

Financial

- How much money do you have?

- What have you done to earn that money?
- What do your current income streams look like?
- What is your current annual household income?
- What non-cash assets do you have (real estate, businesses, etc)?

Health

- How do you feel overall?
- What kind of exercise do you regularly do?
- What is your current weight?
- What age do people think you are when they meet you?
- How is your mental health?
- How is your emotional health? Do you feel at peace?
- If you are religious, how is your spiritual health?

Fun

- What hobbies do you have?
- What were some trips you have been on recently?
- Do you volunteer anywhere regularly?
- What do you do in your free time?

These questions are not exhaustive, so feel free to add more information not covered by these questions. Each answer is a brick in a particular pillar of your life.

This part of the process is very important and should not be rushed. As you begin, I recommend you spend 1 hour on this segment. Then, over the course of one week, set aside 30 minutes a day to read over your list and add or remove topics.

Every item on the list should feel "right" to you and get

you excited!

A fundamental aspect of this exercise is to allow yourself the freedom to dream. Many people struggle to even voice their dreams and aspirations aloud. If you want to start a business and grow it to 10 million USD a year, then do not be embarrassed to list that specifically in your finances column. If you want to travel the world with your family, write it down. Resist the urge to talk yourself out of it and convince yourself of all the reasons why you cannot. Just write it down.

Do not worry about the "how" just yet, we will touch on that in Step 3.

The main goal for this step is to dare to dream. What could your life be like by the end of this season if everything you hope for comes true? So often we ask ourselves, "What if it doesn't work out?" To that, I say: "Well, what if it does?"

Step 2 - Evaluate The Pillars

Your dream home, supported by the 4 pillars of Family/ Friends, Finances, Health, and Fun, is your destination. This is the vision you will spend the next 9 years of your life moving towards with confidence and joy.

Before we crank the engine and really get moving in Step 3, it is critical to pause and make sure each pillar makes sense individually and combines with the others to create a solid and enduring foundation. This is the work of Step 2. We must ensure that all 4 pillars are level and stable and that no single pillar is weaker or longer than the others.

For example, I once had a client who wanted to build a company to rival the largest in the world. However, she *also* wanted to be home for her daughter upon her return from school every day. In addition, she wanted to swim every morning, do yoga three times a week, and have time left to tend to her large garden regularly.

I believe you *can* have everything you want in life, just not at the same time. Remember, life is seasonal. The beauty of winter and the sweetness of summer are each to be enjoyed in their own time.

My client's dream of building a billion-dollar company did not align with her goal of being home for her daughter daily; nor did it fit with having ample time for her gardening hobby. In this example, one pillar was very long and did not align with her other 3 pillars.

Now it's your turn to evaluate. One by one, examine each item in each pillar and make sure they do not conflict with anything in your other pillars.

If there is a conflict, you will have to decide which is more important for you *right now*. This may mean putting one or more goals to the side, at least for the next 9 years. There is nothing stopping you from prioritizing your goals in order of importance in your next 9 year journey.

Step 3 - Make your Life Roadmap

Now that your home is level and stable, you have your destination. Now it is time to make your road map to get there.

Remember, the 4 Pillars represent a foundation for your life 9 years from now. You are now going to use that as a destination and build a roadmap to build clarity on the steps you need to take to get there.

The next milestone on your journey is to figure out where your life needs to be *3 years from now,* to be on track for your life in 9 years.

Will you have started a business? How big will it be in 3 years? Are you married? Do you have kids? What are the kids' ages and how are they doing?

Go through each brick on your 4 pillars list and determine where on the road you need to be in three years, to get to your ideal home at the end of the journey.

Once you have determined your 3 year vision, think 1 year from now. Where do you have to be in 1 year to reach your 3-year goal? As before, methodically examine each Brick one by one.

The final step is to plan for the near term. You take each Brick and break it down into where you have to be 8 months from now, 4 months from now, and then 3 months, 2 months, and 1 month from now.

Here is a worksheet that you can fill out to keep track of it all.

Pillar: _____ Page: ___

9 Year	3 year	1 year	8 month	4 month	3 month	2 month	1 month

Making your map will be more challenging than you expect. A key difference between people who reach their destination and those who do not, is that those who succeed invest time in building their map.

You may find that some of your 9 year goals are not possible while maintaining the other pillars. Again, you may have to sacrifice something from one pillar in order to reach the objectives in another. Keep asking yourself what is most important to you for *this season* until you find your answer.

You may also find that you have not been ambitious enough. If, after completing this part of the exercise, you think "Wow, that looks easy", then you are probably selling yourself short. Go back to your 9-year pillars list and see if you can think even bigger.

This process can take days or even weeks to complete. That is fine, don't rush. Remember to take all the time you need on this step. An investment of a few weeks is nothing when you compare it with the results of having a road map for the next 9 years of your life.

Step 4 - Write your 9 Year Letter

We have arrived at the most important step of all: The 9 Year Letter™ itself.

Using your 4 Pillars and your Life Roadmap as a guide, write a letter to yourself from 9 years in the future. This letter should describe in immense detail the life that your future self has created, as well as the amazing journey you took to get there.

The location for writing this 9-year letter is in the house you built with your 4 pillars. Describe it in sensory-rich detail.

Here is an example of how to start:

"*Dear Ray,*

It's me, or should I say, you, from 9 years in the future. I am sitting here in the office of our beautiful home in the mountains. In the distance, I can see the sunshine reflect off a river down the hill. Laura is playing outside in the garden with Aaron, who is now 12. It's a cool spring day and the flowers that Laura planted are starting to bloom.

I am sipping coffee, a delicious Mexican blend with more milk than coffee. As I write you this letter, I can't help but feel an overwhelming feeling of joy and gratitude. Our life is amazing.

Over the last 9 years, I have built up multiple businesses that now generate income for me almost passively, and I spend most days at home writing and spending time with the family ..."

In the letter, cover everything you wrote down in your 4 Pillars. Talk about the events that happened along the way that led you to where you are today. Spare no detail. How do you feel? Write about both physical and emotional feelings. The secret to the 9 Year Letter™ is to make it all as real as possible to your mind and heart. Make use of the senses that touch our hearts and write to yourself with vivid reference to smell, sight, sound, music, and feeling.

Many people get emotional during this process and that is okay, and even to be expected. This is your dream home and your dream life. Everything you wanted in the next 9 years has worked out.

Once you finish the letter, read it to yourself out loud to make it even more real. If you can muster the courage, read it to your closest and trusted confidants as well.

A tip: Write this letter by hand. This will not only give you time to really live in each moment as you write it out, but it will also establish a physical and emotional connection with each word and thought.

Next Steps

While your next steps may be simple, they also may be the hardest.

You now have a roadmap and you have to follow the steps in your map. You may have some rainy days on your journey and fall behind schedule. Do not let this discourage you. Use good days to get ahead, and accept that bad days happen.

After you have followed through on your road map for the first four months, then do the monthly planning for the next 4 months. When you finish the yearly plan, do another yearly plan. When you finish the 3 year roadmap, then make another 3 year roadmap.

When nine years have passed and you have finished the roadmap, re-read your 9 Year Letter. Try not to be shocked that you have completed everything you set out to do and maybe even more.

The final step in this 9 year season of your life is simply to sit down and write another Nine Year Letter for the next season of your life. Then, take a deep breath and set off on your next journey with focus, clarity, determination, and joy!

Tips to use with clients

For every step of the process, encourage your clients to dig beneath the surface of all their observations. Endeavor to guide your client in understanding the details and the "why" behind their 9-year goals. Sometimes, what they really want is not what they think they want, and it is only by completing each step in detail and asking the right questions that both you as a coach, as well as your client, can write the 9 Year Letter™ that will lead to an ideal and fully actualized life.

Ray Blakney

Entrepreneur, Father, Husband, Accidental Business/Life Coach and semi-professional sword fighter

Website: https://9yearletter.com

Facebook: https://www.facebook.com/raymond.blakney/

Instagram: https://www.instagram.com/ray.blakney

Twitter: https://twitter.com/RayBlakney

LinkedIn: https://www.linkedin.com/in/raymondblakney/

Ray Blakney became a business/life (blife?) coach by accident, despite his best efforts not to become one.

After exiting his 4th company, he was approached by somebody who saw him speak at an event about becoming his coach and mentor. After repeated attempts at politely saying no, Ray tried to convince this person to give up, by giving what he thought was a crazy price for his coaching. To his shock, the person said yes, and Ray became a coach.

Over the next few months, Ray started mentoring this person and assisted in growing his business from just a few hundred thousand a year to over a million.

Since then, Ray has worked with many other clients and found that his mentorship covered more than just work. He found that to help grow a person's business, he also needed to help cast a vision for their life. Over time, others heard what he was doing and approached him to do the same. Thus, the 9 Year Letter Method™ was born.

Complete Your Collection!

Activate Your Life

Vols 1-3

Best Sellers in Personal Transformation

Activate Your Life Vol. IV

25 Transformational Exercises From
Coaches All Over The World

Published by
The Art of Adventure
3631 Hartford Street
Saint Louis, Missouri
Derekloudermilk.com

Edited by Joia Karen Holman
Proofread by Rebekah Tolley-Georgiou

Disclaimer:
This book is not intended as a substitute for the medical advice of physicians.
The reader should regularly consult a physician in matters relating to his/
her health and particularly with respect to any symptoms that may require
diagnosis or medical attention. The information provided in Activate
Your Life is for educational and informational purposes only and is made
available to you as self-help tools for your own use. The Authors cannot and
do not guarantee that you will attain a particular result, and you accept and
understand that results may differ for each person.

TABLE OF CONTENTS

PART 4 - Relationship to Personal Growth and Business Empowerment

PART 5 - Relationship to Inner Goals and Outer Environment

INTRODUCTION

Welcome! This is the fourth volume in the *Activate Your Life* series, and it is a wonderful collection of coaching, healing, and spiritual exercises. Over the years of the Activate series, we have seen the exercises rise to meet the times we are in. As humanity goes through its great awakening process, you will find the chapters within this book to support you, amidst the radical changes humanity and Mother Earth are going through.

Activate Your Life was born as a project to share the work of amazing coaches. I was living in Bali at the time, and many of the initial authors were my mentors, coaches, and healers. I would bring them in to teach sessions at my AdventureQuest retreats, and the experiences they created would blow people away. I wanted a way to bring those experiences to the world, and also help my friends become published authors.

At the time, I was part of a collaborative book project where 100 entrepreneurs shared a key business lesson in their own chapter of, *The Better Business Book*. The book became a bestseller and gave me the confidence to publish my first solo book, *Superconductors*. I realized how a collaborative book project like this could grow community, demystify the publishing world, and build confidence in the authors.

As the host of *The Derek Loudermilk Show* podcast, I see it as my job to bring cutting-edge ideas and thought leaders to my audience, and the *Activate Your Life* book series is a beautiful complement. In *Activate Your Life Volume IV*, you will encounter the leading minds in the coaching, healing, and metaphysical worlds.

When I first started as an entrepreneur more than a decade ago, a few simple exercises changed my life. One such exercise was to envision my perfect day in detail. Three years later, as I was watching the sunset over the Adriatic Sea with my family, I realized that I had just lived out that exact perfect day. Going through just one exercise can truly *Activate Your Life*.

How to use this book

We have broken down the content into different sections with certain themes – I recommend going straight to the section that calls to you, or where you think you will find the biggest benefit.

You can learn something or you can *know* something. You could just read this book and gain new insights and ideas, which is great. But to fully activate and transform your life, to know something, you must have a lived experience - so, these exercises are all about action. You will get the biggest benefit by setting aside some time, and being fully present as you move through the process of an exercise.

It can be useful to remember that when you are working on a transformational process, it can sometimes feel uncomfortable or destabilizing. This is because your brain is working hard to create new connections as you learn. Your worldview, or personal identity, may be shifting, and you may have to use courage and willpower if you face challenging truths. Anytime our physical body or thoughts are changed, it interrupts the careful balance called homeostasis, and this requires energy. Learn to embrace discomfort, because this means the exercises are working!

To keep your momentum, it can help to have a strong emotional attachment, with the outcome you are seeking.

Check back in with *why* you are doing these exercises in the first place. What is the vision you see for yourself? Who needs you to show up and do your best with these exercises?

If you are a coach, welcome! After starting this project, the authors soon discovered that we were excited to learn and use everyone else's exercises. Please feel free to try out, use, and adapt these exercises with your own clients. I've heard from hundreds of coaches that use the *Activate Your Life* books as a reference guide, to find the right exercise for any coaching situation. You can even build out the curriculum for your events and retreats using these exercises. If you would like to republish any particular exercise, please contact the individual author.

This book gives you access to a team of the world's top transformational facilitators, in the comfort of your own home. This is a great book to bring to your mastermind or networking group, or do with an accountability buddy. As with the African proverb, *"To go fast, go alone. To go far, go with friends"*.

You can go far with this book, but if you are truly motivated to transform your life, I encourage you to seek continued support from coaches. All of our authors offer additional training and programs, or 1-1 support. If you want more from a particular coach, please visit their website or email them directly. Contact details will be found in each coach's Biography.

We hope *Activate Your Life Volume IV* will help you break through your most pressing challenges, and guide you to achieve your biggest goals.

The world needs you, now more than ever.

Derek Loudermilk

October 10, 2023

PART 1

RELATIONSHIP TO PERSONAL HEALING